When Ohio Was Blue

BLISS INSTITUTE SERIES

Bliss Institute Series

John C. Green, Editor

Lee Leonard, *A Columnist's View of Capitol Square: Ohio Politics and Government, 1969–2005*

Daniel J. Coffey, John C. Green, David B. Cohen, and Stephen C. Brooks, *Buckeye Battleground: Ohio, Campaigns, and Elections in the Twenty-First Century*

Douglas M. Brattebo, Tom Lansford, and Jack Covarrubias, editors, *A Transformation in American National Politics: The Presidential Election of 2012*

Douglas M. Brattebo, Tom Lansford, Jack Covarrubias, and Robert J. Pauly Jr., editors, *Culture, Rhetoric, and Voting: The Presidential Election of 2012*

William L. Hershey and John C. Green, *Mr. Chairman: The Life and Times of Ray C. Bliss*

Tauna S. Sisco, Jennifer C. Lucas, and Christopher J. Galdieri, editors, *Political Communication & Strategy: Consequences of the 2014 Midterm Elections*

Christopher J. Galdieri, Tauna S. Sisco, and Jennifer C. Lucas, editors, *Races, Reforms, & Policy: Implications of the 2014 Midterm Elections*

Jerry Austin, *True Tales from the Campaign Trail, Vol. 1: Stories Only Political Consultants Can Tell*

William Hershey, *Quick & Quotable: Columns from Washington, 1985–1997*

Joy Marsella, *Creating a New Civility*

William Hershey and Colleagues, *Profiles in Achievement: The Gifts, Quirks and Foibles of Ohio's Best Politicians*

Jerry Austin, *True Tales from the Campaign Trail, Vol. 2: Stories Only Political Consultants Can Tell*

Jerry Austin, *True Tales from the Campaign Trail, Vol. 3: Stories Only Political Consultants Can Tell*

William Hershey, *Taking the Plunge into Ethiopia: Tales of a Peace Corps Volunteer*

Dale Butland, *When Ohio Was Blue: My Twenty-Year Journey with John Glenn*

When Ohio Was Blue

My Twenty-Year Journey with John Glenn

DALE BUTLAND

The University of Akron Press
Akron, Ohio

ISBN: 978-1-62922-322-3 (paper)
ISBN: 978-1-62922-324-7 (ePub)

A catalog record for this title is available from the Library of Congress.

∞ The paper used in this publication meets the minimum requirements of ANSI/NISO Z39.48–1992 (Permanence of Paper).

Cover art: Photo by Ron Kuntz, used with permission of his estate. Cover design by Amy Freels.

Unless otherwise specified all photos appear courtesy of Dale Butland

When Ohio Was Blue was typeset in Minion Pro by Amy Freels.

Produced in conjunction with the University of Akron Affordable Learning Initiative. More information is available at www.uakron.edu/affordablelearning/

The lights begin to twinkle from the rocks:
The long day wanes: the slow moon climbs: the deep
Moans round with many voices. Come, my friends,
'Tis not too late to seek a newer world.
—Alfred, Lord Tennyson

To Vicki and our children: Danielle, Chad,
Brodie, Shane, and Carter.

Contents

Prologue

THAT ALL SEVEN US PRESIDENTS born in Ohio were Republicans might leave a false impression. For most of Ohio's history, the state's politics have been reliably middle of the road, albeit with a slight center-right tilt.

But for a roughly twenty-year period that began in 1974, a humble hero from small-town New Concord and a fiery big-city boy from Cleveland turned the state's political landscape upside down.

John Glenn and Howard Metzenbaum were Democratic giants who paved the way in turning Ohio politics bright blue for nearly a quarter century.

By the 1980s, Democrats controlled every statewide office, both houses of the state legislature, and a majority of Ohio's congressional delegation, as well as commanding a majority on the Ohio Supreme Court.

This aberration did not, however, extend to presidential elections, where Ohio remained, in today's color-coded political parlance, vividly purple.

In the 1970s, Republican Richard Nixon and Democrat Jimmy Carter each carried the state once.

In the 1980s, while Democrats John Glenn and Howard Metzenbaum were winning two terms apiece in the US Senate, GOP presidential candidates Ronald Reagan and George H. W. Bush collectively carried the state in all three of that decade's presidential elections.

In the 1990s, Democrat Bill Clinton won the state in both 1992 and 1996.

And from 2000 to 2012, Republican George W. Bush and Democrat Barack Obama each carried Ohio twice.

In short, even during the Glenn/Metzenbaum years, Ohio maintained its reputation as the nation's quintessential swing state, at least as far as presidential elections were concerned.

But those days—and that reputation—are now long gone.

Donald Trump carried Ohio in both 2016 and 2020 by eight points—and, in 2024, won the state by a landslide eleven-point margin.

That headwind proved too great for three-term Democratic US Senator Sherrod Brown to overcome. After his much narrower four-point defeat in that same election, Ohio is now almost beet red.

Democrats who are loath to admit this reality should consider this: When incumbent (and term-limited) Governor Mike DeWine finishes his final term in January 2027, Republicans will have held the governor's office for thirty-two of the past thirty-six years.

Moreover, Republicans now hold every statewide executive office, enjoy veto-proof majorities in both houses of the state legislature, control six of the seven seats on the Ohio Supreme Court, and have a 2–1 majority in the state's congressional delegation.

Swing state? More like Mississippi, North.

Exactly how this happened—and why—is a subject for another book and another day; there are a multitude of causes too complex to deconstruct here. For now, suffice it to say that Ohio in 2025 is a mirror image of what it was in the 1980s.

But this time, one-party dominance may not be an aberration.

As the 2024 elections clearly demonstrated, support for Democrats among working-class voters—who were once the party's base—has largely collapsed. Unless Democrats can figure out how to get them back, demographics may make Ohio a Republican redoubt for years to come.

Unlike neighboring states such as Michigan, Wisconsin, and Pennsylvania that narrowly went for Donald Trump and the Republicans in 2016 and again in 2024—but were carried by Democrats in the 2018, 2020, and 2022 elections—Ohio has, apart from Senator Sherrod Brown's 2018 reelection, remained firmly in the Republican orbit.

A big reason why is that Ohio's population is older, whiter, and less college-educated than that of those other three states. Ohio's demographic profile, in other words, fits that of the typical Trump voter. And the Trump voter is now the base of the Republican Party.

Moreover, with greater Columbus being the exception, Ohio is *losing* population relative to other states.

Indeed, a 2023 report by the Ohio Department of Development says that if current trends hold, the state's population will fall by 675,000 people—or 5.7 percent—by 2050. In contrast, the US population as a whole will grow by 17.3 percent during that same period.

Who is leaving Ohio? Younger, highly educated people, who are departing the state for better economic opportunities elsewhere.

Who's staying behind? People who are older, predominantly white, less likely to have a college degree, and who, with each passing election, are becoming a larger share of the state's overall electorate.

How—or whether—this demographic trend can be reversed is also a subject for another day.

This book is centered around Ohio politics in the Democratic-dominated 1970s, '80s, and early '90s—and my personal journey with the two men who perhaps best defined that era in Ohio politics, John Glenn and Howard Metzenbaum.

When I say that Glenn and Metzenbaum "best defined that era," I'm not just talking about their partisan affiliation. I'm also referring to how they approached and thought about politics itself—which stands in marked contrast to the apocalyptic, rule-or-ruin dynamic that animates too many of today's politicians and too much of our contemporary political landscape.

For John and Howard, politics wasn't war, opponents weren't treasonous enemies, winning elective office wasn't a license to grift, and losing an election wasn't proof that it was "rigged" or "stolen."

Above all, they knew that compromise isn't "selling out"; it is the way democracy is supposed to work and, in a competitive two-party system, the only way it can survive.

But the era defined by John Glenn and Howard Metzenbaum has, like them, passed away.

And sadly, as I'll outline in this book's concluding chapters, it has been replaced by one whose zeitgeist is not just dark and foreboding but so profoundly dysfunctional that, absent meaningful economic and political reform, we could lose the United States of America we have always known.

Contrary to what Shakespeare told us in *The Tempest*—what's past is not necessarily prologue.

Chapter One
The Journey Begins

I SHOULD NEVER HAVE BEEN in this position.

I didn't have insider political connections or come from a prominent family. In fact, I was just one generation removed from Ellis Island, where two of my grandparents had stepped off a boat to chase the American dream.

I didn't graduate from an Ivy League college.

I had zero experience on Capitol Hill.

Yet here I was in May 1980, hired to write speeches for a United States senator.

And not just any senator.

My senator was a national hero and one of the best-known people on the planet.

My new boss was John Glenn, who became a household name in 1962 when—at the height of the Cold War and the United States' "space race" with the Soviet Union—he crammed himself into a tiny capsule called *Friendship 7*, rocketed through a keyhole in the sky, and became the first US astronaut to orbit the earth.

How I came to work for him was entirely serendipitous.

I had originally come to Washington in late 1978 as a political appointee in the Carter administration, working in the US Department of Commerce's Office of International Trade.

How *that* came to pass was equally serendipitous.

The year before—only a dissertation shy of earning a PhD in political science at the University of Chicago—I landed my first "real" job at the Chicago Council on Foreign Relations (now the Chicago Council on Global Affairs).

As head of the council's "corporate service program," my job entailed bringing high-profile federal officials and policy experts to Chicago to address topics of interest to the council's many corporate members.

One such speaker was Stanley Marcuss, who was then serving in the Carter administration as deputy assistant secretary of commerce for international trade.

In a previous incarnation, Stan had worked in the US Senate and become friends with Geoffrey Shields, another young lawyer who worked on Capitol Hill.

In time, Geoff migrated to Chicago, where he was a partner at a large, business-centered law firm and, fortunately for me, a regular attendee at many of my corporate service programs.

When Geoff learned I was bringing Marcuss to speak at the council, he and his wife hosted a dinner for us at their suburban Chicago home.

Stan and I hit it off instantly and, by the end of the evening, he had offered me a job in Washington as his special assistant.

A few months later, in December 1978, I went to work as a "Schedule C" political appointee at the US Department of Commerce.

Stan was soon promoted to assistant secretary for international trade; we continued to work closely and even coauthored an article in 1979—"Reconciling National Interests in the Regulation of International Business" for the *Northwestern University Journal of International Law and Business*.

By the spring of 1980, however, President Carter's reelection chances seemed dubious.

Though he was leading in the polls—a lead he would not relinquish until the month before the election—American diplomats were being held hostage in Iran, gasoline prices were soaring courtesy of the newly formed OPEC oil cartel, and Senator Edward Kennedy of Massachusetts was in the midst of mounting a strong primary challenge.

Seeing the proverbial writing on the wall, I began circulating my resume on Capitol Hill.

Though I grew up in Maryland, I started with the Ohio congressional delegation because, with my mother now living in Columbus, it was the state where I was registered to vote.

I managed to get a couple of interviews, but no job offers.

As mothers often do, mine came to the rescue.

When my dad passed away in 1974, my mom had to go back to work and soon landed a secretarial position with an AFL-CIO union official.

As word spread that her son was looking for a job on Capitol Hill, one of her labor contacts arranged an interview for me with Bill White, Senator Glenn's chief of staff.

I prepared diligently for that meeting.

Knowing that Glenn served on the Senate Foreign Relations Committee, I tried to sell myself as a potential legislative assistant who had an academic background in international affairs and work expertise in international trade and business.

As White's eyes glazed over, I realized that my interview was obviously pro forma and had only been offered as a courtesy to one of the senator's political allies.

Desperate, I blurted out that I thought I also wrote pretty good speeches.

At that, White suddenly perked up.

"Oh, really?" he said. "Well, we might be in the market for a speechwriter. I'd like to see some samples of your work."

I quickly sent White a few speeches I'd written for Stanley Marcuss, along with the law review article mentioned earlier.

A few days later, I got a call inviting me to meet and interview with Senator Glenn himself.

The interview went well and, before the week was out, I was hired. I started my new job on May 1, 1980.

My title was "Speechwriter and Legislative Assistant for Small Business."

"Small Business"?

As it turned out, Glenn's office was also looking for someone to replace a legislative staffer whose portfolio had included small business issues.

Mine was a classic Washington story, one I often relate to young people who ask me how to get a job on Capitol Hill.

Because DC is a veritable magnet for anyone wanting to work in politics, almost every congressional office attracts stacks of resumes from hundreds of young hopefuls, most of which are never read.

When a job opening arises, it is often filled by someone who walks through the door and happens to be in the right place at the right time.

In politics as in life, timing is everything.

As I said, my hiring was serendipitous.

Inasmuch as my primary job would be speechwriting, my first priority was to familiarize myself with Glenn's speaking style, which entailed researching his past speeches.

What I learned was that while John Glenn was a heroic figure admired for many reasons, delivering memorable orations was not among them.

Tapped to give one of the two keynote addresses at the 1976 Democratic National Convention (when many regarded him as the front-runner to be Jimmy Carter's vice-presidential running mate), John delivered a thoughtful, policy-heavy speech that, to put it charitably, underwhelmed delegates, pundits, and a national television audience.

It certainly didn't help that John's prosaic remarks were followed by a fiery, rhetorical barn burner given by his co-keynoter, Congresswoman Barbara Jordan of Texas, who was not only the first African American, but also the first woman to ever give a keynote address at a National Democratic Convention.

The verdict was swift and devastating.

John Glenn was "dull and boring." And he had literally talked himself out of being Jimmy Carter's running mate.

Reputations are hard to shake in Washington.

Once the national media and pundits tag you, it is exceedingly difficult to erase the label they've assigned.

And now I was the "dull and boring" guy's speechwriter.

While I was proud of having been hired, it was a little like being boxing promoter Don King's barber: It was a bit embarrassing to tell anyone.

In fairness, John's '76 convention speech wasn't as bad as the reviews suggested.

It was merely the wrong *kind* of speech for that audience.

National political conventions should never be confused with university seminars or Ted Talks.

At base, they're mostly an excuse for like-minded partisans, often wearing funny hats and outfits, to get together and yell hurray for us and to hell with the other guys.

In other words, successful political party convention speeches are usually rah-rah exercises: long on applause lines and notably short on scholarly discourse.

Here, it's probably worth explaining how writing speeches differs from other kinds of writing like, say, writing novels or newspaper columns.

When you write a speech, you're writing for the ear.

When you write books or magazine articles, you're writing for the eye.

When you're writing for the eye, the reader—if he or she fails to comprehend or get the point of what's being said the first time through—can go back and read the passage again. Or even a third time.

But when you're writing for the ear, the listener has only one shot at understanding the point being made. If what the speaker says isn't clear the first time around, the listener doesn't get a second chance.

And that is why a good speech will consist of short, declarative sentences and steer clear of long, complicated statements or clauses in which the audience can easily get lost.

Speaking of short, my personal rule of thumb is that formal speeches should rarely, if ever, exceed twenty to twenty-five minutes in length.

The goal is to leave the audience wanting more, not leave them exhausted and wanting the ordeal to end.

When I wrote for Senator Glenn, the organizations inviting him would often tell me they wanted him to speak for forty-five minutes—or even an hour.

I never complied with those requests.

Nobody likes to be bored. And no matter how interesting speakers may think they are, the truth is that the mind can absorb only what the backside can endure. Better to give a shorter speech and then fill whatever time remains in the program with a "question and answer" period that gets the audience actively involved.

Finally, there's the applause line—which is where speechwriters, especially political speechwriters, earn their money.

Most anyone who is reasonably literate can write an expository sentence that intelligently conveys a thought or point.

But not everyone can construct well-crafted applause lines that excite an audience, motivate it to action, or prompt it to clap and cheer.

Applause lines can be funny, inspiring, partisan, or cutting.

But by definition they can't be boring.

That's something I kept top of mind when Glenn agreed to introduce Senator Lloyd Bentsen of Texas—Michael Dukakis's vice-presidential running mate—at the 1988 Democratic National Convention in Atlanta.

Suffice it to say that John's '88 convention speech was entirely different from the one he gave twelve years earlier in 1976.

But more about that later.

When I started working for him in 1980, Glenn was facing reelection to the Senate that fall.

After his blowout maiden win in 1974 (when John carried all eighty-eight Ohio counties), few Republicans were anxious to volunteer for what they saw as the kamikaze mission of trying to deny him a second term.

Which explains why a likable but little-known state representative from suburban Cleveland named Jim Betts evidently drew the short straw at Republican headquarters and was tapped to be the GOP's standard-bearer for the US Senate.

The year 1980, of course, was also a presidential election year.

And since the incumbent president, Jimmy Carter, was not a strong presence at the top of the Democratic ticket (Ronald Reagan ended up beating him in Ohio by half a million votes), you might think—especially if you've grown up in today's politically polarized environment—that Glenn was a lot more vulnerable than he actually was.

But politics in Ohio—and around the country—was entirely different forty-five years ago than it is today.

Back then, few states were either entirely "red" or entirely "blue." And what it meant to be a Republican or a Democrat wasn't the same, either.

In 1980, liberal Republicans and conservative Democrats abounded nationwide.

New York, for example, often sent liberal Republicans like Jacob Javits to the Senate, while Mississippi routinely elected conservative Democrats like John Stennis.

(It should be noted that in the 1970s and '80s the South, in yet another legacy of the Civil War, was still overwhelmingly Democratic. Since Lincoln freed the slaves and was a Republican—indeed, the *first* Republican president—only Democrats were likely to get elected in the former Confederacy for decades thereafter.)

On top of that, in 1980 Ohio was still America's swing state poster child—and Buckeye voters were practiced ticket-splitters. It wasn't at all unusual for Ohioans to cast their ballots for a Republican presidential candidate while also voting for Democratic US House or Senate candidates.

The 1980 election was a perfect example.

While Jimmy Carter managed to capture just 41 percent of Ohio's popular vote, Glenn garnered a whopping 69 percent and beat the hapless Jim Betts by 1.8 million votes—the largest winning margin for a US Senate race in Ohio history.

In the process, Glenn also racked up editorial endorsements from every major newspaper in the state.

Except one.

The Wrong Guy

The *Toledo Blade*, then as now a closely held paper owned and published by the Block family, gave Jim Betts his one and only major media endorsement.

It wasn't until years later that I learned how that came to pass. And the story is a classic example of how adventitious politics can be.

According to *The Blade's* managing editor at the time, the editorial staff all assumed that publisher Paul Block (father of current publisher John Block) would again opt to endorse Glenn as the newspaper had done six years earlier.

Accordingly, and in advance of the meeting at which the endorsement would be finalized, they wrote a draft editorial extolling Glenn and urging his reelection.

At the meeting, however, Block shocked everyone by announcing that he wanted to endorse Betts instead—and gave them twenty-four hours to write the editorial.

"Well," the editor told me, "Jim Betts had a pretty thin list of accomplishments in the Ohio House, but we did the best we could. We then met with Mr. Block the next day to get his final approval for the endorsement that would run that weekend."

After reading the first paragraph or two, Mr. Block threw it down on his desk and thundered that he didn't give a damn about what Betts had done in the *state* legislature, he wanted the editorial to focus on what he'd done as a *congressman*.

"We all nervously shifted around and looked at one another. Finally, I worked up the courage to say, 'But Mr. Block, Jim Betts is a state representative in the *Ohio* House; he's never been in Congress.'"

Block looked at the editorial staff, then looked down at the editorial they'd written.

"Sh**," he said, "I must have the wrong guy. But what the hell, you've already written the editorial and today is Friday—go ahead and run the goddamn thing on Sunday."

And that is how John Glenn came to lose *The Blade's* 1980 editorial endorsement.

Politics can be a quirky business.

~

Fate can be equally capricious.

In December 1980—barely a month after Glenn's landmark reelection—former Beatle John Lennon was shot and killed outside his Manhattan home by a deranged gunman named Mark David Chapman.

Like many of my generation, I was stunned and deeply shaken by Lennon's murder: its bizarreness, its randomness, its utter pointlessness.

Though I'm not sure I could have explained why, it was vitally important to me that Lennon's death be mourned and his cultural impact be publicly acknowledged by those at the pinnacles of power in our society.

And I now had access to one such person.

I came into the office hours early the next morning to write a "floor statement" that I hoped Glenn would deliver in the Senate and thereby be enshrined forever in the *Congressional Record*.

I knew that Glenn was never a Beatles fan and was even less approving of Lennon's politics and antiwar activism.

It therefore came as no surprise when he bluntly asked why I thought he should use his Senate platform to speak out about what had just transpired in New York.

"Because," I said, "the guy who shot John Lennon didn't do it because he hated his music or his politics.

"Lennon was killed for one reason and one reason only. He was famous. People knew Lennon's name. The shooter wanted people to know *his*. When you think about it, Senator, Chapman's victim last night could just as easily have been John Glenn as John Lennon."

The senator looked at me for a moment, then nodded.

And shortly thereafter left for the Senate floor to deliver the remarks I had written.

~

As you might imagine, Glenn's 1980 landslide reelection—by a margin three times larger than Ronald Reagan's in a key swing state—immediately thrust John into the national conversation as a potential 1984 Democratic presidential candidate.

That was fine by John, who was supremely self-confident, entirely cognizant of his status as a national hero, and whose deep ties to the Kennedy family had, I've always believed, made him particularly susceptible to the presidential bug.

Chapter Two
The Glenn-Kennedy Connection

JOHN'S CONNECTION TO THE KENNEDYS was genuine and years in the making.

Though Glenn had, after his orbital space flight in 1962, met and spoken several times with President Kennedy, it was the president's brother and his US attorney general—Robert F. Kennedy—with whom Glenn built a lasting friendship.

I first became aware of how deep that friendship was during my first few months as John's speechwriter, when he often opted to close his remarks by quoting Ralph Waldo Emerson:

> If there is any period one would desire to be born into, is it not the age of Revolution? When the old and the new stand side by side and admit of being compared? When the historic glories of the old can be compensated by the rich possibilities of the new era? This time, like all times, is a very good one, if we but know what to do with it.

I often wondered how and why John came to love that quotation.

One day while the two of us were flying to Ohio aboard his six-seat, twin-engine Beechcraft Baron, I asked.

(A consummate pilot—149 combat missions in two wars, test pilot, astronaut—John routinely flew his own plane to and from Ohio for political and other events. Staff, VIP guests, and Ohio reporters assigned to cover Glenn all got, at one time or another, what I came to call the "copilot treatment": being invited to sit up front with him, donning a headset, twisting the control panel knobs as he instructed, and unfailingly pinching themselves at their good fortune to actually be flying with *JOHN GLENN.*

(A confession: Even after nearly twenty years of "copiloting" with John, I still don't have the foggiest idea of what I was doing or what those knobs and dials I was twisting were designed to do.

(I've never been crazy about flying in small planes, but as I used to tell my wife, Vicki, "If you have to fly in one, you can do worse than have John Glenn as your pilot."

(A major drawback, of course, was if that plane had ever gone down, no newspaper story would have mentioned me until at least the fourth paragraph, which would have begun: "Also on board . . .")

When I asked about the Emerson quote and why he so often insisted on using it, John grew pensive.

"Well," he said, "Bob Kennedy and I became such good friends that our families sometimes vacationed together. And when he ran for president in 1968, I campaigned with him all over the country.

"In fact, Annie and I were with him in Los Angeles the night he was assassinated after winning the California primary.

"Because Annie was feeling a bit under the weather on election night—and we knew the podium would be totally mobbed—we decided to stay in our room at the Ambassador Hotel and watch Bob's victory speech on TV.

"When he was shot, we, of course, dashed to the hospital."

But Bob didn't die immediately, and he and Ethel had brought several of their children with them to LA. The kids had gone to bed before the shooting and were still asleep at the hotel and didn't yet know their dad had been horribly wounded.

"Ethel asked if Annie and I would fly the children back to the family home in Virginia so they wouldn't be subjected to the media frenzy in Los Angeles.

"Naturally, we did.

"That first night back at Hickory Hill in McLean, I wandered into Bob's study. And there on his desk was an open book about Ralph Waldo Emerson that he'd been reading.

"When I sat down, I noticed that Bob had circled a quote that he obviously intended to use himself. Maybe because I was so upset and didn't know what else to do, I memorized it right then and there—and I've been using it in my speeches ever since."

The next day came the call from California that Bob had not survived his wounds.

But because of the three-hour time difference between California and Virginia, the Kennedy children once again were in bed and asleep.

It fell to John to "go into each child's room, wake them up, and tell them their dad wouldn't be coming home."

After a long pause, he added: "It was the hardest thing I've ever done."

John served as a pallbearer at Robert Kennedy's funeral and helped carry his friend's casket to its final resting place in Arlington National Cemetery.

There's another story about John and Bob (Glenn never called him "Bobby"), which he shared with me during a different flight to Ohio, that I think not only reflects how close they were, but also reveals something significant about John's character.

To the best of my knowledge, John never told the story publicly.

But I recounted it in "John Glenn: The Last American Hero?," a *New York Times* op-ed I wrote immediately following John's death in December 2016.

By 1968, John had retired from the Marine Corps and taken a job as president of a major American soft-drink company's international division.

"We were living in New York, and they were paying me $100,000 a year, which at that time was real money," he told me. "For the first time in our lives, Annie and I didn't have to worry about putting our kids through college or helping our parents financially as they got older."

That spring, Bob decided to run for president and Glenn readily agreed to campaign for him. John's employer, however, wasn't keen on having its highest-profile executive publicly supporting Mr. Kennedy.

Unsurprisingly, John was soon summoned to an "emergency meeting" of the corporate board where a resolution was to be passed barring any board member from "engaging in partisan politics in 1968."

When the meeting was called to order, John rose from his seat to say that there was something his colleagues should know before taking a vote.

"Bob Kennedy asked me to campaign for him and I told him I would.

"And I will, because he is my friend.

"And if keeping my word means I can't be associated with this company any longer, I can live with that.

"But if that's what happens, we're going to walk out of this room and you're going to hold your press conference and I'm going to hold mine. And we'll see who comes out better."

No vote was called and the meeting was quickly adjourned.

John's politics, of course, aren't the point of this story.

To me, it was his fierce determination to keep a promise to a friend, even at the expense of sacrificing the first real financial security he and his family had ever known.

It's the kind of courage we don't see much anymore. In politics or anywhere else.

Chapter Three

Glenn's 1984 Presidential Campaign, Part I

JOHN'S STATURE AS A NATIONAL hero—coupled with his huge Senate reelection win in 1980 that demonstrated his appeal to both sides of the political aisle—was doubtless why national polls soon began showing him as the Democrat best positioned to face and possibly beat President Reagan in 1984.

Political pressure swiftly built for John to begin visiting early primary states to prove he had allure *outside* Ohio, which is why we took our first trip to New Hampshire in November 1981.

Needless to say, that trip generated enormous interest back home—and several Washington-based Ohio newspaper reporters accompanied us on the trip.

Today, of course, daily newspapers are dying or barely hanging on by their fingernails.

But there was a time in the not-so-distant past when most major dailies staffed and operated Washington bureaus so they could report national news with a local angle and not have to rely exclusively on wire service reporting.

Though it was still three years before the next presidential election, New Hampshirites were hoping against hope that Glenn might make news by declaring his candidacy. And that gave us an excellent opportunity to have some fun.

We opened John's speech this way:

> It's great to be here in New Hampshire, home of the nation's first presidential primary.
>
> Now I've heard all the talk, especially in Democratic circles, about how the nation might want a new president in 1984 (some nervous, anticipatory laughter from the audience).
>
> And how the best candidate for us to nominate might be someone who comes from America's heartland... maybe someone from the Midwest... someone from a state like, say, Ohio (more laughter, scattered applause).
>
> Maybe even someone who has made his name outside of politics in some great national undertaking like, for example, the space program... (laughter).
>
> ...and someone whom many Americans regard as a national hero (laughter fades as a hush begins to fall over the crowd).
>
> Well, I've heard that talk... and I've taken it very seriously.
>
> So after giving it a lot of thought... after talking with friends and family about what I should do... (audience now totally silent; one could hear the proverbial pin drop).
>
> I've come to New Hampshire to announce... (long pause as the audience now held its collective breath).
>
> That I've spoken with Neil Armstrong—and he's not interested.

With that, the room exploded into laughter and applause... and the rest of what John had to say that night was beside the point and quickly forgotten.

~

It was the first of *many* trips we would make to New Hampshire over the next three years.

Building a presidential campaign is an expensive and difficult proposition.

Ideally, the person at the top—the campaign manager—knows the candidate intimately, enjoys the candidate's confidence and trust, has national campaign experience (or knows people who do), has at least a passing relationship with deep-pocketed donors outside the candidate's home state, is a good judge of political talent, has contacts with and is respected by the national media, and is seen as being up to the job by the professional political class in Washington.

Bill White, the senator's chief of staff turned presidential campaign manager, met only the first two of those criteria.

And as the campaign went on and the performance of the Glenn campaign failed to align with the senator's heady initial poll numbers, pressure began to build for White to be replaced.

Eventually, he was. But not until January 1984.

And when White went, he unfortunately gave way to a gaggle of political hired guns recommended to John by former Democratic National Committee Chairman Bob Strauss, many of whom seemed more focused on hefty paydays for themselves than on Glenn's success in the presidential primaries.

The campaign speechwriting operation was a different story.

As chief speechwriter, I was permitted to hire the personnel I chose—and I remain proud of the team we assembled.

Dennis Fitzgibbons, my first hire, had worked for the legendary Michigan Congressman John Dingle and was superb.

My second hire, Eric Schnurer—then still an Ivy League college student—was and is one of the smartest people and best writers I've ever known.

Despite our age difference (I'm ten years older), Eric and I built and nurtured a friendship of more than forty years that continues to this day. He is among my closest and dearest friends.

I like to think Glenn's speechwriting team was one of the few operations in his presidential campaign that didn't let him down.

But there is only so much speechwriters can do.

Chapter Four
The Gridiron Dinner

IN EARLY 1983, JOHN WAS still riding high in the polls and vying with former Vice President Walter Mondale for the top spot on the Democratic ticket.

Mondale, however, was better known among the Washington elites—and John still had the albatross of his disastrous 1976 National Democratic Convention speech draped around his neck.

In the 1980s, there was a rite of passage for aspiring politicos in Washington, known as the Gridiron Dinner.

Held in a DC hotel ballroom, it was an annual event at which the Washington establishment came together to laugh, spoof, and gently poke fun at one another through song and dance skits and the political version of stand-up comedy.

The black-tie, invitation-only event—attended by top politicians from both parties, Supreme Court justices, cabinet members, and national print and broadcast media heavyweights—was, at least officially, "off the record," though highlights from the night usually found their way into the next day's *Washington Post*.

Though the Gridiron Dinner still exists, the criticism it has received in more recent years (for the alleged "coziness" it engenders among politicians and the journalists who cover them) has diminished much of its cachet.

But in 1983, it was still a very big deal.

Traditionally, the president was one of the evening's top two speakers—and being asked to represent the opposition party was a coveted invitation. (At the '83 Gridiron, President Reagan at first begged off but then made a "surprise" appearance and promptly upstaged the evening's nominal Republican keynoter, Senator Bob Dole of Kansas.)

For the person representing and speaking for the party out of power, it was something of a high-wire act.

Succeeding—or bombing—on that big stage in front of Washington's mightiest movers and shakers could and often did leave a lasting impression.

That presumably is why former Vice President Mondale—who received the initial invitation to be the Democratic keynoter—turned it down.

Glenn was the Gridiron's second choice—and he immediately accepted.

Not everyone thought it was a wise decision.

Legendary *New York Times* political pundit James Reston (known to friends and insiders as "Scotty") even wrote a nationally syndicated column in which he pronounced Glenn's acceptance of the invitation to be a "mistake."

John had many wonderful qualities, Reston wrote, but giving a funny speech wasn't one of them.

Because everyone inside and outside the Glenn campaign knew the stakes were sky high, in no time at all we were able to assemble a dream team of well-known and experienced Washington humor writers to help me craft Glenn's remarks.

That team included nationally syndicated columnists Art Buchwald (like Glenn, a former marine) and Mark Shields (who had once worked for former Ohio Governor Jack Gilligan), along with former RFK staffer and veteran Washington hand, Dick Drayne.

Our Gridiron team met after work, several times a week for a month, in Glenn's Senate office conference room.

It was a highlight of my Senate career—and I don't think I've ever laughed that much before or since. Jokes and topics for jokes flowed as freely as the beer we drank with the carry-out pizza we often had for dinner.

The synergy generated by the comedic talent in that room was truly electric; ideas bounced, played, and built off each other and the humor came in torrents.

Alas, some of what I thought was our best material was so raunchy or pointed that it couldn't actually be used at the Gridiron, which had an unwritten policy against the use of "blue" humor and a formal policy against anything too caustic ("The Gridiron singes," its slogan went, "but never burns").

About a week before the dinner—which was held on Saturday, March 26—we had what we needed. It then fell to me to organize and wordsmith the material into a script, which I then brought back to the team for refinement and editing.

Two days before the dinner, we presented John with a final draft and urged him to practice on his own before we would all meet at Buchwald's house on Saturday morning for a final run-through.

Buchwald had a podium set up in his dining room, and the rest of us sat in chairs facing Glenn as his "audience."

When giving a speech, John had an ingrained and irritating habit of adding ad-libbed and extraneous words to whatever text he was using.

For most speeches, that wasn't a major problem, though it did interrupt the flow of otherwise carefully crafted words and often weakened the impact of declarative sentences and applause lines.

It was, however, John's way of making speeches written by others "his own."

In fact, I always thought it was part of Glenn's love/hate relationship with the job I was hired to do for him—the clearest expression of which came in a comment he made to my mother after she congratulated him on his remarks at a political dinner we all had just attended.

"Thanks, Helen," John said, "but you know I'm actually just Charlie McCarthy to Dale's Edgar Bergen."

It was a lighthearted but nevertheless uncomfortable reference to one of America's most famous ventriloquists and his "dummy."

Given Glenn's closeness with the Kennedy family, I always found it odd that he was so sensitive about speaking words he didn't pen himself.

While it is true that some Ohio political reporters wrote stories or columns about the improvement in John's rhetoric since I was hired, it is equally true that *none* of the Kennedy brothers felt the least bit awkward about giving speeches whose most memorable lines had been drafted by others.

President Kennedy's best speeches were written by the incomparable Ted Sorensen; Robert Kennedy used Sorensen and Dick Goodwin; and Ted Kennedy's words were crafted by the transcendently talented Bob Shrum, with whom I later became friends.

But nobody thinks of Ted Sorensen when they hear "Ask not what your country can do for you; ask what you can do for your country." They attribute those words to John F. Kennedy.

Nobody thinks of Bob Shrum when they hear "The work goes on, the cause endures, the hope still lives, and the dream shall never die." They think Ted Kennedy.

As they should. The words in a speech are properly seen as belonging to the speaker (whether elected official or corporate CEO) because that person chose to speak them.

Speechwriters are simply employees, no different in kind from all the other assistants and aides who work for politicians and business bigwigs.

Automotive executive Lee Iacocca, for example, is known as the "father of the Ford Mustang" because he—not the engineers who designed the car—brought it to market. And he—not they—would reap the public credit (or blame) for how the car was received by the public.

In any event, when the Gridiron Dinner team gathered at Art Buchwald's house for the rehearsal, Glenn again began adding extraneous words to the script we had given him.

But this time, Glenn's ad-libbed words were deadly to the mission and what we were trying to accomplish.

Humor fundamentally depends on timing—and a joke completely loses its punch and fails to be funny if random words are thrown in between the setup line and the punch line.

John was only about five or six lines into his rehearsal when Buchwald stood up and said, "Wait a minute, John. Stop. What the hell are you doing?"

Glenn looked puzzled. "What do you mean? I'm reading my speech."

"No," Buchwald said, "you aren't. You're adding a bunch of words to the jokes and you're f***ing the whole thing up. Just read what we wrote, OK?"

It was all I could do to keep from shouting "amen."

Buchwald's rebuke was what I had so often wanted to say to John myself—but obviously couldn't.

Buchwald, however, was a friend of John's, a fellow combat veteran, and a peer.

He was also a celebrity in own right and a volunteer.

He was not, in other words, a staffer on the senator's payroll.

After glaring at Buchwald and the rest of us for a moment or two, Glenn began the speech again, this time reading it precisely as written. He was terrific.

That night at the Gridiron, John blew the doors off the place.

To his credit, in all the years I worked for Glenn, he was never afraid or hesitant to use self-deprecating humor—and instinctively seemed to understand its utility. Nothing wins an audience over faster than a celebrity willing to laugh and poke fun at himself.

"As some of you may know," he began, "Scotty Reston thinks it was a mistake to accept this invitation because I can't give a funny speech.

"So after reading his column, I turned to [former DNC Chairman] Bob Strauss for some advice.

"He said, 'John, don't worry. Just give the same speech you gave at the '76 Democratic Convention. The whole damn country laughed at that one.'"

The audience roared... and John was off to the races.

Joke after joke hit home and was met with laughter and applause; he had the crowd in his pocket.

Midway through, Glenn paused, peered out at the audience until he spotted Reston—and then delivered, seemingly offhand, one of our better lines: "How am I doing, Scotty?"

As everyone assumed he would be, President Reagan was also excellent that night. As a former movie actor, the Great Communicator had few equals when it came to polished oratorical performances.

But John, who no one predicted would even hit a double, had now unexpectedly hit a grand slam.

After the speech—feeling certain that he finally had the "dull and boring" monkey off his back—Glenn's feet were barely touching the ground as we walked to his car in the parking lot.

At which time he revealed that Buchwald, Shields, Drayne, and I had inadvertently created a monster.

"You know," John said without a trace of self-awareness, "I thought Reagan was pretty good tonight."

Pause.

"But I thought his timing was a little off, didn't you?"

Chapter Five

Glenn's 1984 Presidential Campaign, Part II

ONE OF THE CRITICISMS OF Glenn's ill-fated presidential campaign—and, in my view, a fair one—was that he had largely failed to offer a persuasive rationale for his candidacy or explain exactly why he wanted to be president.

And after John's disastrous fifth-place finish in the Iowa caucuses and a weak third-place showing in the New Hampshire primary a week later, everyone knew the campaign was in deep trouble. The only way to avoid a death spiral, if that were even possible, was to somehow stop the bleeding.

The campaign decided that the first step had to be a pugnacious and candidacy-defining speech—and that the place to do it was at Boston's historic Faneuil Hall, the venerable "cradle of liberty," where Revolutionary War patriots often met to galvanize their cause.

I decided to write that speech alone—and worked on it for days.

It began with Glenn's lifelong commitment to the nation, recalling how he had proudly "fought and flown" for America in two wars and as our first astronaut to orbit the earth.

The bulk of the speech laid out John's motivations for running, his vision for the country, and what he specifically hoped to accomplish on issue after issue, including his determination to

> build a future in which our country finally and forever lays aside racism, sexism, and every other "ism" that divides and cripples us—and works to make the old dream of justice a new American reality.
>
> It is a future in which America's relations with the rest of the world reflect neither a retreat into isolationism nor a march into militarism—and where we earn respect not just for the power of our arms but also for the strength of our ideals.

It ended with a defiant rebuke of media pundits who had already declared his candidacy dead after just two primaries: "So to those whose vision is confined to yesterday's polls and who say that the contest for our Party's nomination is over, I reply: The people have not yet spoken—and the race has just begun."

The crowd—packed in like sardines at Faneuil Hall—gave John's rallying cry a standing ovation, and the speech earned positive media coverage, both nationally and in Ohio.

But one speech does not a campaign make. And our numbers in the ensuing primaries did not improve.

The resulting collapse of Glenn's presidential campaign (he failed to win a single primary, finished second in only one, and dropped out in March shortly after "Super Tuesday," but not before running up a $2 million loan debt to four Ohio banks that haunted him for years thereafter) has been adequately dissected elsewhere by more objective authors than I—and there's no reason to retread that well-plowed ground in this book.

Here, I'll say only that Glenn was not an ideal presidential candidate.

His political moderation (which he described as "the sensible center") does well in general elections, but isn't well suited to primary fights largely decided by party activists.

Moreover, Glenn was not a good administrator, was far less demanding of his staff than he should have been, often delegated responsibility almost to a fault—and then had little interest in following up on key campaign decisions or on how well they were being carried out.

I loved John Glenn and admired him immensely.

If being president required only coolness under fire, wisdom, and sound judgment in crisis situations, I have no doubt he would have been a good, maybe even a great, one.

But the skill set required to be a good president is much broader than that and is entirely different from the skill set required to be a good presidential candidate.

Unfortunately, John lacked many of the skills necessary to be either one.

Worse, however, was that his embarrassing flame-out in that 1984 presidential campaign threatened his reelection to the Senate two years later.

There were two reasons for that: The first is that the political landscape is littered with the political corpses of US senators who ran for president, lost, and then got tossed out of office by their home state voters the next time they were up for reelection.

I'll address how we dealt with that shortly.

Right Stuff; Wrong Staff

But Glenn's presidential campaign itself—and the advice he got from some of the "expert" hired guns he was dependent on—also could easily have cost him reelection to the Senate.

Let me offer a representative example.

As a senator, Glenn had a perfect, 100 percent voting record on the issue of civil rights.

Indeed, early in his first term (in 1978, before I started working for him), he courageously challenged the Senate's hypocrisy in exempting itself from many of the nation's laws, including the Civil Rights Act of 1964.

Harshly characterizing his place of work as "the last plantation," Glenn urged his Senate colleagues to drop their double standard and obey the same laws and rules they imposed on everyone else—and, specifically, to outlaw discrimination in hiring and promotion based on race, color, religion, sex, or national origin.

Though he got little traction with the issue as a freshman senator, years later—as chairman of the Senate Committee on Governmental Affairs—Glenn held hearings designed to eliminate the Senate's self-serving artifice.

And in 1995, his efforts finally bore fruit when Congress passed the Congressional Accountability Act, which applied thirteen different civil rights, labor, and workplace safety laws to the legislative branch.

Glenn's championing of civil rights was a major reason why African Americans and other communities of color overwhelmingly supported him every time he ran.

Yet late in his presidential campaign—just prior to Super Tuesday and the day before Glenn's last debate as a presidential candidate—the hired guns, led by the late Greg Schneiders, a former DC bar owner and adviser to Jimmy Carter who somehow managed to win Glenn's trust and worm his way into the role of campaign press secretary, scheduled him to give a speech at, of all places, Georgia's infamous Stone Mountain.

For those who may not be familiar with the landmark, the granite-like monument at Stone Mountain (now a state park just a few miles east of Atlanta), which features bas-relief carvings of Jefferson Davis, Stonewall Jackson, and Robert E. Lee on horseback, has long been known as a memorial to the Confederacy and was a favorite site for Ku Klux Klan rallies.

The symbolism was not subtle. The campaign "brain trust" had decided that playing the race card was how they would position Glenn to win Super Tuesday's southern state primaries.

The next morning, I arrived in Atlanta where I was to be part of the debate prep team.

When I confronted the senator in his hotel room with the "Stone Mountain story" from the front page of that day's *Atlanta Journal-Constitution*—and asked how in the world he had agreed to this—he was devastated.

"Honest to God, Dale, I'd never heard of Stone Mountain and didn't know what it was."

I believed him then and still do.

Later that day, I approached the hired guns and asked how they could have put the senator in that position.

One of them, Bob Albers, merely shrugged and said, "The question is: Do you want to win or not?"

Breathing fire, I said, "No, you sons of bitches, the question is even if John *could* win that way—which he can't—what kind of Democrat would *want* to win that way?

"You know as well as I do that this campaign is over. John Glenn won't be president, but he's still going to be a United States senator from Ohio—where, by the way, he has a 100 percent voting record on civil rights. How in the hell is he going to explain giving a speech at Stone Mountain?"

"That's not our problem," one of the dolts replied.

I had to restrain myself from decking all of them.

The issue—John's commitment to civil rights—was not just a political one for me. It was also personal—and one of the reasons I wanted to work for him.

Kirby

In 1971—the year after I graduated from college at Abilene Christian University in Texas—the Taylor County juvenile officer, for whom I had done volunteer work as an undergraduate psychology major, retired.

I applied for the job and on December 14, 1971, became, to the best of my knowledge, the youngest county juvenile officer in the history of the state.

I was twenty-two years old.

But if I was the youngest juvenile officer in Texas history, I probably also had the shortest tenure in office.

In April, just four months into my new job, a young Black youth who was then about eleven years old (whom I shall identify only by his first name, Kirby) got into trouble when he and a friend "stole" a car and drove it a few blocks before getting out and running away.

I knew Kirby from my student days, when he regularly showed up at my off-campus apartment and asked if there were any chores he could do for my roommate and me in exchange for feeding him dinner.

He came so often that one day I asked in exasperation, "Kirby, don't you ever eat at home?"

To which he replied, "My mamma's too drunk to cook."

I came to find out that Kirby's brother was in prison, he never knew his father, and his mother reportedly sometimes worked as a prostitute to make ends meet.

Being familiar with the young man's rancid domestic situation, I knew he couldn't remain in that home.

But I also did not believe he belonged at Gatesville, the horrific and almost medieval youth reformatory, which is where my boss, Domestic Court Judge Henry Strauss, told me he was headed.

A good alternative, I thought, was Boys Ranch, a local nonprofit institution funded in part by United Way that took in and tried to salvage wayward youngsters guilty of only nonviolent, relatively minor offenses.

After being informed by one of my office associates that "the Boys Ranch doesn't take ni**ers," I met with Strauss and suggested I quietly visit with Boys Ranch administrators, explain my personal knowledge of Kirby's situation, and politely remind them that United Way did not permit racial discrimination at the institutions it funded.

"Now, Dale," the judge said, "we don't want to alienate the Ranch. They've helped us out so many times in the past. And we all know things don't change overnight."

As retrograde as that may sound today, remember that this was 1971—in a state that had been part of the Confederacy.

After thinking it over, I concluded that I could not in good conscience be complicit in sacrificing the children I was sworn to protect on the altar of racism.

A few days later, I submitted my resignation, giving the county two weeks' notice.

As it happened, I had previously been scheduled to give a speech at McMurry College on April 22, three days before my resignation became effective. (Abilene, then a town of about 100,000, was home to three different church-affiliated colleges: Abilene Christian, affiliated with the Church of Christ; McMurry, a Methodist school; and Hardin-Simmons University, a Baptist institution.)

I decided to honor my speech commitment, and alerted the local newspaper—the *Abilene Reporter-News*—that I would have a few things to say about the county's indulgence of racism.

The ARN sent a reporter, and the result was a front-page story on April 23 that quoted me extensively—and which promptly got me fired the same morning, two days before my resignation was to be effective.

Though I hadn't mentioned the Boys Ranch by name in my speech (referring to it only as "a certain local institution"), Ed Wishcamper, the managing editor of the *Reporter-News*, invited me to meet and fill him in on the details.

To his credit, the editor then assigned a reporter to investigate the situation at the Ranch which, a few days later, resulted in *another* front-page story headlined "No Blacks at Ranch."

For a relatively sleepy town like Abilene, it was as though a bomb had gone off.

Tempers flared, dueling letters to the editor were published, the Ranch was in retreat.

And I began getting late-night death threats over the phone.

"Hey, Nig**er-lover," one caller said, "How'd you like to get a bullet in your f***ing head?"

I left Abilene a few months later to begin graduate school studies.

But the story had a happy ending.

Less than a year after leaving my job as juvenile officer, I was informed by a friend that the Boys Ranch had finally opened its doors to Black youths—and that Kirby was one of the first kids of color to be admitted.

In hindsight, I now realize that blowing the whistle on racism—fifty-five years ago in the deep South—was a breathtakingly risky proposition. Especially for a fresh-out-of-college, twenty-two-year-old who was born and raised in the North.

But perhaps this story makes it easier to understand why John Glenn's 100 percent civil rights voting record in the Senate was so important to me—and why I was so incensed by the travesty at Stone Mountain during his presidential campaign.

Chapter Six
Press Secretary

WHEN JOHN ENDED HIS PRESIDENTIAL campaign in March 1984, the hired guns, as is usually the case, immediately scattered to the winds.

Though most were superfluous in a Senate office and would not be missed, Glenn's sudden loss of a press and media operation created a hole that obviously had to be filled.

With a national search for a new press secretary already underway, I asked to meet with the senator in late spring—and then audaciously explained why I thought I was the right person for the job.

It was a bold (and, I'm sure, entirely unexpected) move that many other senators would have laughed off and rejected out of hand.

After all, I had no experience, no academic or professional background in journalism, and no long-standing relationships with either the national or Ohio press corps.

Instead of summarily dismissing my proposal, however, John said he wanted to think it over.

The next day—in a decision that fundamentally changed the trajectory of my career and professional life—the senator said, "I don't know if it will work, but I'm willing to give it a try. Let's do this: You take the job—and we'll assess how well it's going three months from now."

I was ecstatic—and spent the next few weeks meeting with every member of the Washington-based Ohio press corps, as well as calling political reporters and editorial writers at every Ohio daily newspaper, television and radio station to introduce myself.

I also spent a lot of time becoming familiar with John's positions on every legislative and political issue I could think of.

Next, I hired a deputy press secretary—Martha DiSario—a gifted publicist who was working in the House of Representatives and had strengths I thought would complement mine.

I've often said that being a press secretary is a dilettante's dream: You don't have to know a lot about anything; you need only know a little about everything. After all, the biggest part of my new job was not only explaining John's policy positions, but why he held them.

Three qualities are essential to being a good press secretary.

One is being able to explain even complicated issues in simple, easy-to-understand terms or, as I often counsel other newly minted press secretaries, "explain it like you would explain it to your mother."

The second essential skill (at least when daily newspapers were a huge part of the media landscape) is being able to visualize how what you say will look in print.

Oftentimes, something that sounds fine and politically harmless when you say it in person or over the phone looks terrible on the printed page, where emphasis, irony, and tone of voice can't be captured or used to mediate meaning. Unfortunately, there's no such thing as a sarcasm font.

Having worked with many aspiring press secretaries over the years, I'm not sure the ability to foresee how something you say will look on the printed page is a skill that can be taught. Like political savvy, it's something you either have or lack.

Finally, and perhaps most important of all, there is something that's probably best expressed as a "don't."

Don't lie.

Under any circumstances.

Period.

As a press secretary, credibility is your most important asset.

Once you're caught in a lie (or, almost as bad, caught denying the obvious), your credibility is gone and the media will never again fully trust you.

And that means you're no longer of much use to your boss or your organization.

You can certainly try to put the best face on the facts (or "spin," as it's often known).

You can try to change the subject.

Or if you need time to think, you can tell a reporter you'll call him or her back.

But never lie.

One more rule of thumb for aspiring press secretaries: When the news is bad, be proactive and don't wait for the media to discover it on their own, at which point you'll be on the defensive.

Get the story out yourself—first, and in its entirety. However painful this may be in the short run, it will be far less damaging than the drip, drip, drip that comes from bad news trickling out over an extended period of time.

In short, always go for the quick bleed rather than the slow hemorrhage.

It's a lesson everyone should have learned in the Watergate scandal over fifty years ago. It is truly puzzling that so many politicians, corporations, and organizations still haven't.

As Senator Glenn's press secretary, my first major foray on the national stage came later that summer when I accompanied him to the 1984 Democratic National Convention in San Francisco.

Almost all of Ohio's major daily newspapers and television stations sent reporters to cover it, and they were hungry for interviews with Ohio's senior senator, which I happily scheduled for them.

Among those reporters was the newly hired Bertram de Souza of the Youngstown paper *The Vindicator* for whom, like me, the '84 convention was his first major assignment.

I arranged a one-on-one interview for Bert in the senator's hotel suite, which he and his newspaper were able to bill as an "exclusive" interview for their readers in the Mahoning Valley.

Bert greatly appreciated this small favor—and the goodwill it engendered served the senator well when Bert became *The Vindicator*'s chief political columnist and, later, its editorial page editor.

Dodging Disaster

Two stories from that convention are worth relating. That they both concerned people of Asian heritage (or, in the case of Connie Chung, a Chinese American television broadcaster) is almost freaky.

On our second day in San Francisco, Ms. Chung (then an NBC television correspondent) approached the senator and me at the convention and asked for an interview.

Ms. Chung led us across the convention floor toward a quieter spot she had found. The senator was behind her, one of Ms. Chung's producers behind him, and I brought up the rear in what must have looked like a news conga line.

Suddenly, Chung stopped dead in her tracks and looked at her waist, where a battery pack belt she was wearing was belching white smoke and flames, threatening to engulf the dress she was wearing.

Chung was panicking, frantically twisting her torso as if engaged with a hula hoop.

As bystanders skittered away, Glenn sprang into action—grabbing the belt, unbuckling it, and throwing it to the floor where it burned up harmlessly; typical Glenn, who was always at his best in a crisis that called for quick thinking.

Chung, for her part, was awed and kept referring to the senator as "my hero."

A day or two later, John and I were in a hallway outside the convention where he was taking questions from Ohio reporters in a media scrum.

I always carried a small tape recorder with me to capture Glenn's answers in case he was ever misquoted.

When the news conference ended and I turned my recorder off, one veteran reporter from *The Cincinnati Enquirer* stayed behind to ask Glenn a question (which I only partially heard and have now forgotten) about the Korean War.

John, of course, had been a fighter pilot who earned the nickname "MiG-Mad Marine" for shooting down three Soviet-made North Korean planes in the closing days of the war.

What I *did* hear clearly was Glenn using the word "gook."

And when I saw that the reporter's tape recorder was still on, my heart nearly stopped.

Glenn finished his answer and bade the reporter good-bye before making his way back into the convention.

I stayed behind, not exactly sure what to say to the reporter, but knowing I had to think fast.

"So," I finally said, "you do know that the private conversation you just had with the senator was off the record, right?"

For the uninitiated, *nothing* that is said to a reporter is "off the record" unless both parties agree to make it so. And the agreement must be struck *before* the comment or comments in question are uttered.

I knew that, and I knew the *Cincinnati Enquirer* reporter knew it, too.

He turned off his recorder and looked me in the eye.

"If you're asking me if I'm going to burn him, you can relax. I'm not."

Both the senator and his neophyte press secretary dodged a bullet that day.

When I told Glenn what had happened, he had no memory of using the racial epithet.

That he did use it doubtlessly sounds to younger ears now (as it did to mine then) like a textbook racist *faux pas* that stood in stark contrast not only with John's civil rights voting record, but with what I know he deeply felt about racism and those who use racist language.

I concluded it was a generational thing; a throwback to a time and a war in which such insensitive language was used to insult enemy combatants rather than to demean or dehumanize an entire race of people.

In the twenty years I worked for him, I never once heard Glenn utter another racially tinged remark—and I know he would never have dreamt of using "gook" in connection with anyone he knew of Asian descent.

That's why I always came back to the Korean War explanation.

But human beings are complicated—and often bundles of contradictions. And I know John was genuinely embarrassed to have used that language.

Why Would I Choose to Be Gay?

Perhaps another story will better flesh out what I'm trying to say.

In 1982—during John's campaign for president—there was a piece of legislation before Congress that was commonly referred to as the "gay civil rights bill," which would have prohibited discrimination against gays and lesbians by adding "sexual orientation" to the list of ascriptive characteristics (race, creed, color, and national origin) that were already protected in law.

Initially, Glenn refused to support it. It was one of the few times in my nearly two decades with him that I adamantly disagreed with a position he took.

That John never himself discriminated against gays or lesbians in either his Senate office or presidential campaign (Bob Farmer, our national finance director, was openly gay) made his position on the bill all the more confounding.

In John's view, homosexuality was a "choice" or a "preference"—which he believed made it different from one's race, color, or ethnic heritage. And for that reason, he opposed adding sexual orientation to our civil rights laws.

Though I and others on his Senate staff repeatedly tried to change his mind about the issue, John wouldn't budge.

Until he did.

During his run for president, it so happened that the man who chaired our campaign in New York was a state senator whose district, as I recall, included Greenwich Village.

Once his gay and lesbian constituents learned of Glenn's position on the gay civil rights bill, they demanded our New York chairman do one of two things.

The first was to change Glenn's mind on the issue.

If that wasn't possible, they expected him to resign from Glenn's presidential effort.

And if he did neither of those things, the state senator's gay constituents made it clear they intended to beat him the next time he was up for reelection.

This, of course, put him in a tough spot, especially since he had already spoken to Glenn about the issue and gotten the same response that we staff members had.

In desperation, he told Glenn about the ultimatum he'd been given and asked if John would at least agree to meet with some of the more prominent gay and lesbian people in the senator's district.

Glenn readily agreed, and a meeting was scheduled at the Waldorf Astoria hotel in New York City.

The state lawmaker invited perhaps a dozen people to meet with Glenn, all of whom were accomplished and financially successful in law, medicine, architecture, and other professions.

After welcoming everyone, our senator/host suggested that John begin by explaining why he wasn't supporting the gay civil rights bill—and then open the floor to questions.

Glenn dove right in, laying out his belief that while discrimination was wrong, sexual orientation was a choice or a preference—and that while he believed everyone had a right to make that choice, he simply wasn't convinced that it belonged in our nation's civil rights laws.

When he finished and opened the floor to questions, there was dead silence in the room.

Finally, an African American woman—an attorney by profession—rose from her seat.

"Senator Glenn," she said, "I'm Black. And I'm a woman. Why in the world would I *choose* to be gay?"

The room exploded in laughter.

John laughed too, the tension was broken and, at the end of the meeting, he promised to continue thinking about the issue.

A couple of weeks later, John changed his mind on the gay civil rights bill.

The meeting in New York, he said, got him thinking about his own sexual orientation.

He realized that he himself never "chose" to be straight; he was heterosexual for as long as he could remember; it wasn't something he "preferred"—it was simply the orientation he was born with and he was no more capable of changing it than he was the color of his skin. If this was true for him, it was equally true for everyone else.

And that, he concluded, destroyed any justifiable rationale for discrimination—at least insofar as the civil law is concerned.

Though the Supreme Court's *Obergefell v. Hodges* decision legalizing same-sex marriage wasn't handed down until 2015—long after John had retired from the Senate and just a year and a half before he passed away—we talked about it and I know he supported the ruling.

As an elder in the Presbyterian Church, he was certainly aware that many people of faith oppose same-sex marriage on religious grounds.

And he steadfastly believed that no court or governmental body should be allowed to tell a church what marriages it will bless or must recognize within its community of believers.

At the same time, however, John also believed that no church should be able to impose its own sectarian rules on the larger civil society.

In other words, Glenn firmly supported the separation of church and state.

On one occasion, I remember discussing the fact that the Roman Catholic Church, for example, does not recognize divorce and remarriage except within narrowly prescribed circumstances.

But divorced Catholics who remarry outside the church are still *legally* married, and their unions are subject to the same civil laws, benefits, and privileges enjoyed by those whose vows were church-sanctioned. Nor does the Catholic Church deny or try to change this reality.

On what basis, then, should the state—which, under the US Constitution, must remain religiously neutral—be able to legally discriminate among its own citizens?

How can the government deny to some citizens the benefits of marriage—ranging from tax breaks to hospital visitation privileges—for reasons that are religiously derived?

We also discussed the absurd notion that all heterosexual marriages—even if they take place in churches or other quasi-religious venues—are "sacred" simply because the spouses are of different sexes.

Can anyone assert with a straight face that the church-sanctioned serial marriages practiced by politicians and Hollywood movie stars—let alone the hasty rituals performed in the middle of the night by Elvis-impersonating "ministers" in "wedding chapels" on the Las Vegas Strip—are somehow more serious, sacred, or worthy of legal recognition than the unions of same-sex couples (like Ohioans Jim Obergefell and John Arthur) who have been in monogamous relationships that often span years or even decades?

John's change of position on gay rights and same-sex marriage was entirely in keeping with his lifelong commitment to civil rights.

And it clearly showed his willingness to change his mind when confronted with new facts or persuasive arguments he had not previously considered.

It was one of the things I loved most about him.

Chapter Seven

Preparing for Glenn's 1986 Senate Reelection Campaign

HAD JOHN NOT RUN FOR president in 1984 and lost, we probably would not have been overly concerned about his Senate reelection prospects in 1986.

But because of the failed presidential campaign, two things were now true.

First, John was more clearly defined as a Democrat in the minds of Ohio voters.

Although he was a lifelong member of the Democratic Party (his parents had been among the few Democrats in the small town of New Concord where he grew up), most Ohioans knew John first and foremost as a national hero.

Veterans revered his exploits as a fighter pilot in World War II and Korea—and *everyone* was aware of his heroism as an astronaut when he gave our country a much-needed boost of confidence during our Cold War space race against the Soviet Union.

In that sense, John previously had almost *transcended* partisan politics.

But in running for the White House, Glenn not only criticized Ronald Reagan, a sitting Republican president who was wildly popular among conservative voters, but also took positions on many controversial issues that underscored Glenn's own Democratic partisan affiliation.

Second, John's aura of political invincibility was now punctured.

Since 1972, there had been a host of US senators who unsuccessfully ran for president and then lost their Senate seats soon thereafter; among them were Vance Hartke of Indiana, George McGovern of South Dakota, Frank Church of Idaho, and Lowell Weicker of Connecticut.

Minding and mending fences in Ohio, we thought, was the surest way to keep that from happening to John in 1986.

Toward that end and whenever the Senate was out of session, Glenn spent much of 1985 back in the state. And by accepting nearly every speaking invitation offered to him, he managed to visit most of Ohio's eighty-eight counties, many of them multiple times.

In those speeches, we put John's embrace of self-deprecating humor to good use, and did not shy away from addressing the elephant in the room.

Whether he was headlining a county Democratic Party dinner or speaking to a local Chamber of Commerce, John typically began his remarks by poking fun at his failed presidential campaign.

> Well, that campaign didn't turn out like I'd hoped, but I want everyone to know that it wasn't my fault.
>
> It was all Annie's fault.
>
> For years Annie told me she wanted me to run for president in the worst way possible.
>
> So that's exactly what I did.
>
> But you know, I'll always be deeply grateful for the wonderful support I had from my family. My wife Annie was always at my side; my daughter Lyn often campaigned with us—and even my son, Dave, took time off from his medical practice in California to help out.

> As some of you may know, Dave's an anesthesiologist—he puts people to sleep. And you know what they say: like father, like son.

And the one-liners kept coming.

> I'm deeply indebted to all of you for being here tonight. Then again, thanks to my presidential campaign, I'm deeply indebted to almost everyone.
>
> Take the four Ohio banks that loaned my campaign two million dollars, for example. I remember them saying, "You know, we really have to give John Glenn a lot of credit." And unfortunately, they did.

Beyond the humor, of course, we were anxious to show Ohioans that even though John had run for president, his ego was still in check. And while he didn't take himself too seriously, he took his responsibilities as their senator very seriously.

He loved the job, never forgot where he came from, and was still someone they could trust to represent them with integrity and common sense.

Videos and a Pornographic Magazine

In Washington, I also looked for new and innovative ways to boost Glenn's profile back in the state.

These, of course, were the days before the advent of cell phones, laptops, social media, and all the other forms of digital communication we now take for granted.

Back then, it simply wasn't possible for politicians to bypass traditional media and communicate easily and directly with their constituents.

Newspapers were still widely read, and radio and television were pretty much the sole means of electronic news dissemination.

Newspapers, however, were fast on the way to losing their primacy in the world of political information, and television (primarily broadcast television) was increasingly the medium through which most people received their news about politics and public affairs.

When the US Senate announced that it was now able to use communications satellites in space to transmit electronic video images to local TV stations around the country, I made sure that ours was among the first Senate offices to jump aboard that bandwagon.

Every major city in Ohio (and even some smaller ones) had at least one television station; many had three, affiliated with each of the three major national networks: NBC, ABC, and CBS.

But because few local television stations had the resources necessary to fund and staff a Washington bureau, the national news they were able to broadcast was wholly dependent on the "feeds" they got from the networks.

With the Senate's new technology, however, it was possible for me to deploy a "government cameraman" to videotape any news conference John held in DC.

Thereafter, I would lightly edit that video in the Senate studio, write a press release on the topic being covered that day, and then fax the release to all Ohio television stations, together with the satellite coordinates they could use to download the video if they wished to use it for a story in their evening newscasts.

For the stations, it was easy-peasy. They needed only to point their satellite dishes at the proper coordinates during the five-to-ten-minute "window" that our feed would be available, download the transmission, and decide whether or not to do a story on it.

I knew, however, that most television newsrooms would be extremely sensitive—if not outright hostile—to the idea of airing as "news" anything that even vaguely smacked of propaganda. The key, then, was to capture the essence of the news conference with footage that was as raw and unedited as possible.

In other words, the goal was to give these stations video that looked virtually identical to what they would have gotten themselves had they covered the event with their own reporters and cameras.

I also was always quick to emphasize that the stations were not only free to make their own editorial judgments about what was "newsworthy," but to edit the video we provided in any manner they chose and to use it or not use it as they saw fit.

This being television news—and *local* television news at that—I also realized that what we provided had to have visual appeal and that anything boring, dry, or excessively complicated stood little chance of making it to air.

Unsurprisingly, the press conference videos aired by the greatest number of Ohio TV stations were about things news hardliners might sniffily call "fluff"—topics which, while interesting to viewers, would never be mistaken for serious discourses on weighty national or international issues.

"Wagers" between senators whose home state teams were squaring off against one another in big-time sporting events were enormously popular.

The annual Ohio State–Michigan college football game, for example, always generates huge interest in both states. Arranging a bet (which typically consisted of the losing team's senator having to wear the winning team's jersey, cap, and "colors" at a postgame press conference) between John and one of his Senate colleagues from "that state up north" was always certain to attract interest from local TV stations and their viewers.

Judged by the number of stations that aired my video feeds, one non-sporting event particularly stood out: Glenn's response to porn-king publisher Larry Flynt's headline-grabbing stunt of sending a complimentary copy of *Hustler* magazine to every member of Congress.

Flynt—whose X-rated career began in Ohio, where he operated a number of strip clubs—obviously was hoping legislators would overreact so he could accuse them of being insufficiently supportive of the First Amendment.

When John's copy of *Hustler* arrived in our Senate mail, I immediately called a news conference, which we held in "the swamp"—an area on the east lawn of the Capitol closest to the Supreme Court, and a favored site for outdoor media events.

We used two props: a lectern and a trash can that was sitting beside it.

"As you may have heard," John told the swarm of Ohio reporters who couldn't resist covering something that seemed vaguely risqué, "Larry Flynt has sent a copy of his disgusting magazine to every member of Congress."

Holding his *Hustler* aloft, Glenn said, "Mr. Flynt says he has a First Amendment right to do this—and maybe he does.

"But I'm here to remind Mr. Flynt that as a United States senator, I too have some First Amendment rights. And one of them is to put this piece of garbage exactly where it belongs: in the trash can."

And with that, John dramatically dropped the magazine into the wastebasket next to his podium.

Needless to say, it was a public relations bonanza for us.

And ratings gold for local TV stations.

Chapter Eight
The Glenn/Metzenbaum Rapprochement

THE EVENT I AM MOST proud of orchestrating involved a far more serious matter and occurred shortly after I became press secretary.

In early June of 1984, a newspaper editorial attacking Ohio's junior senator, Howard Metzenbaum, appeared in the ultraconservative *Washington Times*, which was then owned by an international media conglomerate founded by the Reverend Sun Myung Moon, leader of the cultish Unification Church.

Titled "Sen. Metzenbaum's Red Face," the editorial—ostensibly an attack on Metzenbaum for having accepted a fee for arranging a real estate transaction—was a double entendre, inasmuch as it was written in tandem with a syndicated column published in the newspaper that same day which not only dredged up decades-old allegations of Metzenbaum's supposed communist associations when he was a young man, but actually referred to the senator as "an unrepentant Stalinist."

Upon reading the column, I marched into Senator Glenn's office and urged him to make a speech on the floor of the Senate defending Metzenbaum.

"And why would I do that?" Glenn asked.

Anatomy of a Feud

To understand his question—and before getting to what John actually said on the Senate floor that summer day—some background is in order concerning the frosty and often openly hostile relationship that had existed for years between the two men.

It stemmed from the fact that Glenn and Metzenbaum had run against each other—*twice*—in Democratic primaries.

The first time was in 1970, when Metzenbaum was attempting to retain the Senate seat he'd held for a year after Ohio Governor John Gilligan appointed him to fill out the unexpired term of Republican Senator William Saxbe, who had vacated it to become attorney general in the Nixon administration.

Glenn had always planned to run for the Senate himself in 1970 and deeply resented what he considered the unfair advantage Metzenbaum had received through Gilligan's appointment.

Usually, taking on a sitting senator of your own party is a heavy lift.

But with Glenn's heroic 1962 orbital flight still fresh in the memory of Ohio voters, he had far greater name identification than Metzenbaum and many political observers thought John was likely a shoo-in.

But Metzenbaum simply ran a better campaign and unexpectedly defeated Glenn in the primary by a single percentage point.

In November, however, Ohio voters returned that Senate seat to Republican hands when Metzenbaum narrowly lost the general election to the GOP's Robert Taft Jr.

Four years later—in 1974—Glenn and Metzenbaum squared off again in a Senate primary, but this time John returned the favor by beating Howard—and then went on to thrash Cleveland Mayor Ralph Perk in November by winning every single one of Ohio's eighty-eight counties, a feat that has never been duplicated.

In 1976, Metzenbaum finally won his own election to the Senate in a rematch with Taft.

But the 1974 primary between John and Howard was a bitter and angry affair that left a years-long legacy of bad blood between the two men.

It stemmed from Metzenbaum's ill-advised attempt to use Glenn's background in the military and space program against him.

First, Metzenbaum tried to capitalize on lingering anti–Vietnam War sentiment by constantly referring to his opponent as "Colonel Glenn."

That John never served in Vietnam (he fought in both World War II and Korea) evidently was a minor detail.

Second, Howard sought to contrast his successful career in private business with Glenn's public service credentials by saying John had "never worked for a living" and "never held a job."

It is always politically risky to go after a military veteran.

When your target is also a national hero—and you never served in the military yourself—it borders on political suicide.

Glenn's devastating rejoinder came at what was then Ohio's most hallowed and consequential political debate forum, the City Club of Cleveland.

Traditionally held a week or so before closely contested elections, the City Club debate received extensive coverage in the state's many daily newspapers and was also broadcast live by dozens of Ohio radio stations.

> "Howard," Glenn said, "I can't believe you say I have never held a job. I served 23 years in the United States Marine Corps and fought in two wars. I flew 149 missions and my plane was hit by anti-aircraft fire on 12 different occasions.
>
> "I was also in the space program. (And in both of those jobs) it wasn't my checkbook that was on the line; it was my life that was on the line. Those weren't nine-to-five jobs where I could take time off to take daily cash receipts to the bank.
>
> "Howard, I ask you to go with me, as I went the other day, to a veterans' hospital and look at those men with their mangled bodies... and then look them in the eye and tell them they didn't hold a job.

"You go with me to any Gold Star Mother, and you look her in the eye and tell her that her son didn't hold a job.

"You go with me on Memorial Day, and you stand in Arlington National Cemetery where I have more friends than I care to remember, and you watch those waving flags... you stand there and you think about this nation... and then tell me that those (brave men) didn't have a job.

"I tell you, Howard Metzenbaum, you should be on your knees every day of your life thanking God that there were *some* men in this country—*some* men—who DID hold a job. And their self-sacrifice is what made this country possible.

"I have held a job, Howard."

~

In that moment, the election was over.

Metzenbaum was toast.

It became official a few days later when Glenn won what had previously been a close primary by eight percentage points.

But the larger takeaway is that the Glenn/Metzenbaum contests were not run-of-the-mill, vanilla primaries; they were rough, mean, and intensely personal.

Simply put, the two men did not like each other.

In fact, they despised one another.

And their mutual loathing manifested itself in the way each tried to one-up the other after they became colleagues in the US Senate.

Even in such low-stakes matters as the Senate's co-ed summer softball league.

Most Senate offices fielded teams with tongue-in-cheek names.

Senator Edward Kennedy's squad was called the "Boston Ted Sox."

Howard's team was known as "The Amazin' Metz," while John's was named—what else—"The Right Staff."

Most games were good-natured fun, with the winners and losers joining each other for laughs and a few beers at a local bar following the contests.

But not the annual Glenn/Metzenbaum softball game.

It was the one and only game each year when *both* senators not only showed up, but actually played themselves (Glenn pitched; Metzenbaum was a "DH," or designated hitter).

The senators' antipathy for one another was mirrored by their staffs; tempers flashed, "out" and "safe" calls were hotly disputed, and the games were always knock-down, drag-out battles with both sides doing everything they could to win, both legal and illegal.

"Ringers," for example, were routinely employed.

Just weeks after I joined his staff, Glenn groused to me about Metzenbaum's alleged softball perfidy, musing aloud about how maybe he should call Rafer Johnson (a one-time Olympic athlete and RFK aide whom Glenn had come to know during Kennedy's 1968 presidential campaign) and ask him to play in the upcoming Ohio showdown.

As it happened, I had been a pretty good baseball player myself and had even played a summer of semiprofessional ball in Louisville, Kentucky. I sometimes wondered if that part of my resume was the *real* reason Glenn had hired me so quickly.

If so, it paid off. In the years I played, The Right Staff never lost a game to The Amazin' Metz.

Or at least that's how I choose to remember it.

~

In light of all this history, perhaps John's query when I suggested he defend Howard against the *Washington Times'* red-baiting editorial—"and why would I do that?"—is a bit more comprehensible.

Glenn had not yet seen the editorial or its accompanying syndicated column.

Handing the newspaper to him, I stood by while he read it in silence.

He laid the paper on his desk and contemplated for a moment before saying, "You're right. This is way over the line. Howard deserves better. Write me a floor statement."

I returned to my press office, polished the remarks I had already written before our meeting, and got John's final review and signoff.

I then called the Washington-based Ohio press corps and told them Glenn would be going to the Senate floor within the hour to make a statement about Metzenbaum—which all but guaranteed that every one of them would be in the Senate gallery.

My final call was to Roy Meyers, Howard's longtime press secretary.

When I told him Glenn was about to speak publicly about his boss, there was a long pause.

"What's he going to say?" Myers finally managed to ask.

"I think you'll be pleased" was the only preview I gave him.

Taking the floor of the Senate about forty-five minutes later, Glenn said in part:

"It has been a blessedly long time since Washington has witnessed character assassination by innuendo. But unfortunately, that destructive tradition has now been revived on the pages of *The Washington Times*.

"And how else can one characterize the accusation that Senator Metzenbaum is an 'unrepentant Stalinist'? Such journalism is tawdry, offensive, and a slander on the reputation of a United States Senator who has served the people of this nation with courage and distinction.

"Senator Metzenbaum and I have had our differences. But he is a loyal, patriotic American who deserves far better than to be smeared with this kind of warmed-over McCarthyism."

Following his speech, Glenn had not been back in our Senate office for more than ten minutes before Howard called to thank him profusely.

A day or two later, John held a fundraiser at a Washington hotel to help retire the debt that was left over from his presidential campaign.

Metzenbaum showed up unannounced and gave John a personal check for $1,000.

A few weeks after that, Metzenbaum offered to serve as honorary chairman of John's 1986 reelection campaign; an offer Glenn quickly and gratefully accepted.

The feud was over.

It was a new day in Ohio politics.

And the state's two Democratic senators would henceforth work together as never before.

Two years later, John returned Howard's political favor and served as honorary chair of Metzenbaum's final reelection campaign.

And at Howard's request, John agreed to let me take a nine-month leave of absence from my Senate job to serve as communications director for the 1988 Metzenbaum reelection campaign—a topic I'll address in much more detail later in this book.

Chapter Nine

A Rose Is a Rose and Glenn's 1986 Reelection Campaign

BEFORE MOVING ON TO JOHN'S 1986 Senate reelection campaign, I want to share a story that occurred in September 1985 when baseball great Pete Rose of the Cincinnati Reds—who died in 2024—broke Ty Cobb's all-time Major League hit record.

As a baseball fan all my life (John wasn't, despite having had Boston Red Sox Hall of Famer Ted Williams serve as his wingman during the Korean War), I knew that Rose collecting his 4,192nd hit was a monumental event—and nowhere would it be a bigger deal than in Cincinnati, a baseball-crazy town that was also the largest city in what was then the most Republican part of the state.

With John scheduled to be on the ballot the following year, I figured a good word to Rose from Ohio's senior senator would be both good manners and good politics.

The morning after Rose broke the record, I suggested that the senator get Charlie Hustle on the phone and congratulate him. John asked me to dial him up.

Going through the Reds' switchboard, I soon had Rose on the line (he'd been up all night in the clubhouse fielding—ahem—calls from all over the world).

"Mr. Rose," I said, handing the phone to my boss, "please hold for Senator Glenn."

John put the call on "speaker" so I could listen to both ends of the conversation.

"Pete," he began, looking at the notes I'd written, "I'm calling to congratulate you on your incredible achievement. 4,192 hits. Wow! And you broke Ty Cobb's all-time record. I can't imagine how great you must be feeling right now."

"Thanks, Senator," replied Rose, who had a well-deserved reputation for not being the brightest bulb in the chandelier. "It's really something. And you know, I'm pretty sure I'm feeling just as good as you did when you walked on the moon."

I had to stifle a laugh and turn away, but John didn't miss a beat.

"Well, you've set a record that may last forever—and I just want you to know that all Ohioans are mighty proud of you today, Pete. I don't want to keep you because I know you've been up all night, and I imagine you're pretty tired. So please get some rest—and again, my heartiest congratulations."

"Thanks, Senator, thanks for calling," Rose said as he hung up the phone.

Who could have dreamed that just four years later—in 1989—Pete Rose would be found culpable for betting on games—including some he had played in or managed—and be punished with a lifetime ban from Major League Baseball—a ban that was only lifted in 2025 after his death.

~

Thanks largely to the success of John's home state fence-mending efforts in the wake of his failed presidential campaign, his 1986 reelection to the Senate was never really in doubt.

His Republican opponent, Congressman Tom Kindness from western Ohio, was largely unknown outside his district, didn't raise a significant amount of money, and never posed a serious threat.

As a result, there was no need to build a large campaign organization, which mostly consisted of a campaign manager (improbably named Rupert Ruppert), a scheduler, a pollster, our paid media consultant, and me, in the role of campaign communications director.

~

A *Jeopardy!* Detour

In fact, John's polling lead over Kindness was so significant that we were even able to squeeze in some out-of-state fundraising events to help retire Glenn's presidential debt, including a trip to California early in 1986 that, oddly enough, resulted in my being a contestant on the television game show *Jeopardy!*

At the time—the iconic Alex Trebek had just taken over as the show's host a couple of years before—auditions were held in person and only at their Los Angeles studios.

Though I was unfamiliar with the show and had never watched a single episode, Martha DiSario, my deputy press secretary, thought I was good with trivia and took it upon herself to call *Jeopardy!*, ascertain that an audition would be held on one of the dates John and I were scheduled to be in Los Angeles and, of her own accord, sign me up for a tryout.

I passed the written and oral tests and, several months later, was offered a spot as a contestant. I accepted and paid my way back to LA for the October tapings.

To say I was no Ken Jennings would be a gross understatement. I won exactly one game, finished second in another, and left town with $1,000 in cash, an all-expenses-paid trip to New Orleans, and some "lovely parting gifts" provided by the show's corporate sponsors, which included (I'm not making this up) several packages of fake fingernails and a year's supply of pancake syrup.

I mention all of this only because my *Jeopardy!* appearances, which aired in January 1987, provided some welcome comic relief at a fateful time during Howard Metzenbaum's 1988 reelection campaign. But more on this later.

When election day in 1986 rolled around, Tom Kindness managed to carry a few counties, nearly all in or adjacent to his congressional district. But Glenn won in seventy-seven of Ohio's eighty-eight counties, captured more than 62 percent of the popular vote, and romped to a third term in the Senate.

From Press Secretary to State Director

Following the election, I told John that I was thinking seriously about running for Congress myself—probably in 1990—and wanted to move to Columbus, which had been my voting address since my parents relocated to Ohio years earlier.

Obviously, I needed time both to build local political connections beyond those I had through Senator Glenn and to raise my own visibility in the city and congressional district I would seek to represent.

Glenn graciously allowed me to relinquish my press secretary duties and named me his state director to manage and oversee constituent services in his four state offices located in Columbus, Cleveland, Cincinnati, and Toledo.

For those who may not be familiar with how congressional offices work, legislative matters are exclusively handled in Washington, while constituent problems pertaining to federal matters and programs (such as Social Security, Medicare, the IRS, the Small Business Association, and immigration) are handled by their state offices.

Though passing legislation—along with the heated political battles which often accompany it—generates news headlines, the political importance of effective "constituent services" cannot be overstated.

Most voters, after all, never actually meet their senators and congressional representatives or talk with them about the issues of the day.

Voters' only contact, if they have any at all, with the people they elect to represent them occurs when they have a problem with a federal agency and turn to their senator or congressional representative for assistance.

Whether or not they have a positive experience—and how effectively their problems are resolved—can go a long way toward determining their vote in the next election.

Another job of a senator's state chief of staff is to represent the senator at the many events that the officeholders themselves cannot attend.

Often, that involves speaking on the senator's behalf; meeting with business, labor, and community leaders on matters that concern them; and generally serving as the boss's "eyes and ears" back home in the state.

For my purposes, the job description was a perfect fit—even though, after my first marriage imploded in 1989, I ended up deciding not to run for Congress after all. It was one of the few unfulfilled dreams of my life. But at the time of my divorce, my three sons were aged six, four, and two—and I saw being a dad as simply more important than being in Congress. I've never regretted the choice I made, even for a moment.

I moved my then-intact family to Columbus in early 1987, Glenn hired a new press secretary, and I thought my time in Washington—at least as a Senate staffer—was over.

Turns out I was wrong.

~

L'Affaire Keating

In April, a group of five senators—Glenn, John McCain and Dennis DeConcini of Arizona, Don Riegle of Michigan, and Alan Cranston of California—met with federal regulators on behalf of a Cincinnati-based businessman named Charles Keating who was under investigation for directing the bank he owned (Lincoln Savings and Loan) to violate various investment rules.

In particular, the feds believed Keating might have steered accounts insured by the Federal Deposit Insurance Corporation (FDIC) into risky commercial real estate ventures—which would leave taxpayers on the hook if those ventures went south.

Though Keating had been a prominent figure in Cincinnati (both as a businessman and for the role in he played in heading up various local anti-pornography efforts), Glenn didn't know him particularly well nor count him among his supporters.

Moreover, Keating and his business empire had decamped for Arizona in the 1970s, which further truncated his ties to Ohio.

But John had a problem: His 1984 presidential campaign had ended about $3 million in debt—$2 million of which was owed to four Ohio banks, each of which had loaned the campaign $500,000 just weeks before Glenn withdrew from the race.

As every politician can attest, raising money for an upcoming campaign isn't easy.

Raising money to retire a debt from an election that's already over is even more daunting—especially if you lost.

Not that John didn't try.

He held fundraiser after fundraiser.

He triaged the debt so that mom and pop vendors and other "little guys" who weren't owed very much were paid off first.

He also made sure that the four Ohio banks got their $2 million back, and were thus repaid for every penny of the principal they loaned his campaign.

And even though federal campaign finance laws strictly limited the amount of money candidates who received federal matching funds could put into their own campaigns to $50,000 (which Glenn had contributed early on), he petitioned the Federal Elections Commission to allow him to pay off the rest of his campaign's debt personally, promising in return never to run for president again.

The FEC turned him down.

Moreover, even though all four banks offered to write off the interest that had been steadily accruing on their loans, the FEC refused to allow that either, saying such forgiveness would constitute an illegal corporate contribution to Glenn's campaign.

The upshot was that John was left in a Catch-22 campaign debt limbo; he couldn't raise the money he needed from others—and he was legally barred from paying it off himself.

It hung like an anvil around his neck... and seemed destined to stay there in perpetuity.

Enter Charles Keating, who sent an emissary to meet with Glenn's administrative assistant—Mary Jane Veno—with a pledge that Keating would help the senator retire the debt.

Despite his (at the time) sterling reputation as a successful entrepreneur, some of us were deeply skeptical.

Not only was Keating a Republican who had never previously raised a dime for Glenn, but he now lived in Arizona and no longer had any overt connection to Ohio politics.

And then there was his deep involvement years earlier with *Citizens for Decency Through Law*, a Cincinnati-based anti-pornography and anti-gay rights organization that advocated censorship and often traded in outright bigotry.

Why his sudden interest in helping our boss?

But Veno, who had been tasked with finding a way to retire the presidential campaign debt, was looking for any port in a storm.

She wasted no time in introducing Glenn to Keating's emissary. And soon the emissary, Veno, and even Keating himself were planning presidential campaign debt retirement events.

Naturally, it wasn't long before Keating asked for a favor.

Federal regulators, he said, were treating him unfairly.

Though he claimed to have done nothing wrong, they had been investigating him for months, putting him and his businesses under a cloud of suspicion.

Perhaps if Glenn and some of his Senate colleagues were to meet with the regulators, they might be moved to bring their interminable investigation to some kind of conclusion.

In April 1987, at Keating's request, the five senators met with the regulators.

Glenn swore (and a subsequent investigation by the Senate Ethics Committee's special counsel did not dispute) that he urged the investigators only to "either charge Keating or get off his back."

And when the investigators told the senators that Keating was the subject of a *criminal* probe, John said, "I closed the file folder in my lap" and ended his participation in the meeting.

Soon, however, the Senate Ethics Committee would begin a formal inquiry into the actions of the "Keating Five."

Following a twelve-month investigation by Washington superlawyer Robert Bennett (who had been hired as "special counsel"), the committee held a series of public hearings that began in late 1990 with Glenn and the other four senators in the dock.

Those hearings were what brought me back to Washington for several months as Glenn's temporary press secretary.

John wasn't happy with the work being done by my successor and didn't think she was up to the challenge posed by the hearings.

So for several months, I flew into Washington on Monday mornings, served as Glenn's spokesperson for the balance of the week while living in a hotel room, and then flew home to my family in Columbus on the weekends.

But the outcome of those hearings will have to wait a few pages.

Because between 1987 when the senators met with the Keating investigators and the 1990 Ethics Committee hearings, there was 1988—the year I worked for Howard Metzenbaum, and the year John Glenn got an opportunity to shed his "dull and boring" reputation with a primetime speech to the Democratic National Convention in Atlanta.

Chapter Ten
"On Loan" to Howard Metzenbaum

IN JANUARY 1988, PETER HARRIS, Senator Metzenbaum's chief of staff, called to ask when I would next be in Washington and said he'd like to meet with me as soon as possible. As it happened, I was scheduled to be in DC the following week, and we agreed to have lunch.

After a brief exchange of pleasantries, Peter got right to the point.

Metzenbaum, he said, was facing not only the toughest reelection campaign of his career, but the highest-profile Senate reelection campaign in the country.

His opponent would be George Voinovich, the popular Republican mayor of Cleveland.

And the Republican Senatorial Campaign Committee had already signaled that Howard sat at the very top of their target list.

Huge amounts of money would be spent on both sides.

Peter was going to run Metzenbaum's campaign—and the race was sure to be rough and tumble.

If Glenn would agree to it, Howard wanted me to be his campaign communications director.

I was stunned. "Why me?" I asked.

"Because you've got a great relationship with the Ohio press corps, and Howard thinks you're the best political spokesperson in the state," Peter answered.

"But I've just moved my family back to Ohio," I countered, "and don't really want to spend the next year back in Washington."

"Not a problem," Harris assured me. "Metzenbaum's campaign will be based in Cleveland and the state Democratic Party has already agreed to let us rent space for a satellite office in their Columbus headquarters where you will be located."

"But I need my Senate salary," I protested, "and I'm not sure if Senator Glenn would even go for this."

"Metzenbaum will talk with Glenn," Harris said, "and if John agrees, you can take a leave of absence from the Senate and we'll put you on our campaign payroll at a higher salary than what you're currently earning."

"I don't even know Senator Metzenbaum," I said. "I need some time to think about this."

We agreed I'd call Peter in a couple of days with my decision.

I returned to Ohio and, after reflecting on what was at stake, realized how important it was to keep both of Ohio's Senate seats in Democratic hands, especially in a presidential election year when Republicans could retain the White House.

I telephoned Harris to say I'd do it—and Metzenbaum called Glenn immediately thereafter.

John agreed to "loan" me to the Metzenbaum campaign and let me take a nine-month leave of absence from the Senate. But he wanted me to return to his staff right after the November election.

I joined the Metzenbaum reelection campaign on March 1, 1988.

For most of the ensuing months, the Senate was in session back in Washington, which meant that Metzenbaum's campaigning was restricted to weekends when he'd return to Ohio for various political events.

For most of those weekends, our campaign "entourage" consisted of just Howard and me crisscrossing the state as I drove him from one event to the next.

When you're cooped up in a car with someone for eight to ten hours a day, you get to know them pretty quickly.

At the beginning, however, I didn't know Senator Metzenbaum at all—and wasn't sure I'd like him once I did.

Happily, that question was answered early on, just a couple of weeks after I'd joined the campaign.

Knowing that George Voinovich was likely to make an issue out of Howard's personal wealth (Metzenbaum had risen from selling razor blades and flowers outside the Ohio State football stadium while he was a student to making a fortune from real estate investments and founding APCOA, then the world's largest airport parking lot company), Peter Harris and I decided that publicly releasing the senator's income tax returns would be good politics.

Though Glenn had always released his federal tax returns, Metzenbaum had never done so, even though he paid an enormous amount in taxes and his charitable contributions were extremely generous.

To convince Metzenbaum he should do it, Peter decided that when I was driving the senator around the state the following weekend, I should show him the press releases I wrote when making Glenn's returns public each year.

Those releases were simple and largely consisted of four columns: The first was the gross amount of income John earned; the second was the dollar amount he paid in federal taxes; the third was the *percentage* of income paid in taxes; and the fourth showed the dollar amount of charitable contributions he and Annie made.

Behind the wheel of our car with Metzenbaum in the passenger seat, I handed him the tax material and waited as he read it in silence with his glasses perched on the end of his nose.

Leafing through five years of these press releases (like Howard, John had also risen from humble beginnings to become a millionaire after he and a business partner bought a Holiday Inn in Orlando, Florida, that became a gold mine a few years later when Disney World opened nearby), Metzenbaum finally muttered under his breath, "Christ, Glenn's got almost as much money as I do."

"Yeah," I said, never taking my eyes off the road, "Not bad for a guy who never held a job, eh?"

Metzenbaum's head jerked toward me and I thought he was going to explode.

Instead, he started to laugh.

"That was the dumbest goddamn thing I ever did in politics—and John shoved it right up my ass, beat me with it, and I deserved to lose."

The man's got a sense of humor, I said to myself. I think I'm going to like him.

And indeed, I did.

~

The Short-Sleeved Shirt

Before returning to my adventures in the Metzenbaum campaign, however, permit me to take a brief digression into John's friendship with his aforementioned business partner, Henri Landwirth. Its genesis, I believe, provides another telling glimpse into John's fundamental decency.

In the early days of the space program, the original seven Mercury astronauts trained near Cape Canaveral, which was then a sleepy, undeveloped Florida backwater with few bars, restaurants, or other outlets for leisure activities.

It wasn't long, however, before the Mercury 7 men discovered the small Starlite Motel in nearby Cocoa Beach that had a swimming pool and was managed by a young immigrant from Belgium who readily agreed to let them use it anytime they had a day off.

In time, the astronauts learned that Landwirth, the motel manager, and his family had spent several years in Nazi concentration camps, including Auschwitz. Though their parents had died in the Holocaust, Henri and his sister miraculously survived.

Initially separated from one another, the siblings managed to reunite shortly after Europe's liberation in a tale so harrowing and unlikely that it could easily be mistaken for a Grade B movie script.

After making their way to America, Henri served his newly adopted country during the Korean War and then used the GI Bill to take a course in hotel management in New York before landing the motel manager's job in Florida.

Though it is a story John rarely shared publicly, he told me how he and Henri became friends after meeting at the Starlite's pool.

"Back in those days, short-sleeved Ban-Lon shirts were fashionable," John told me, "and all the astronauts wore them when we visited Henri's motel pool."

"But Henri never swam and he never wore Ban-Lon; even when it was incredibly hot, he'd wear a long-sleeved shirt with his bathing suit.

"One day, Henri decided to take a dip with us. And when he took off his shirt, I noticed there were numbers tattooed on his right arm.

"When he got out of the pool and was drying off, I sat down next to him.

"'You know, Henri,' I said, 'if I had numbers on *my* arm, I'd wear them like a medal.'

"When he came out to the pool the next day, Henri was wearing a short-sleeved Ban-Lon shirt. It was a pretty emotional moment for both of us."

After John's orbital flight, the two men stayed in touch and their friendship deepened.

And as it turned out, Henri was a brilliant businessman with a special gift for hotel management. The two hotels he and John bought together (both of which Henri managed) ultimately made them very rich men.

John Glenn and Howard Metzenbaum were very different people with very different backgrounds, personalities, religions, strengths, and weaknesses.

But they had a lot in common as well.

Though Howard was a city boy and John hailed from a small town, they each grew up in families hard hit by the Great Depression.

They were devoted family men who had warm, wonderful spouses and marriages that endured beyond their diamond anniversaries.

They both had delightful senses of humor and core convictions they refused to compromise.

Above all, they loved this country, devoted most of their adult lives to public service, and deeply believed that politics was, in Bobby Kennedy's famous formulation, "a noble profession."

Unlike John, however, Metzenbaum could be a stern taskmaster who did not tolerate mediocrity, accepted no excuses, and demanded excellence from those who worked for him.

I suspect that's a big reason why his Senate staff was widely regarded as one of the best on Capitol Hill.

But even though he was a tough employer, Howard's staff absolutely revered him.

In fact, of all the Senate staffs I came to know during my nearly two decades in Washington, only Senator Ted Kennedy's was as fiercely loyal to the boss as was Metzenbaum's.

Howard's demanding nature extended to his campaign staff as well.

One time, we arrived for an event in Dayton and the room wasn't set up to the senator's liking.

The speaker's podium wasn't big enough to accommodate multiple media microphones, the "Metzenbaum for Senate" banners weren't conspicuous enough, and there was too little campaign literature laid out.

Peter Harris had flown in from Washington to join us on this trip, and Howard asked the two of us to meet him in the hallway.

"Who the hell was responsible for organizing this event?" Howard asked.

When Peter gave the senator a name, Metzenbaum said, "I want her fired. Immediately."

"We can't fire her," Harris replied, "she's a volunteer."

"Well, her volunteering days are over," the senator retorted as he stalked back into the event.

Harris and I looked at each other and suppressed smiles.

Later, Peter spoke with the volunteer and pointed out the deficiencies in her work. She apologized, said it was the first event she'd organized, and promised to do better in the future.

And she did.

At our next event in Dayton, Metzenbaum congratulated and thanked her for a job well done, apparently not recognizing her as the volunteer he had previously demanded be banished from the campaign.

Howard was also the only politician I ever worked for who actually *liked* fundraising.

Glenn, by contrast, absolutely hated asking for money and often said he'd "rather wrestle a gorilla."

Metzenbaum saw it as a challenge to be met and a game to be won.

And he was relentless at it.

If we were running a few minutes early on our way to an event, Howard would often ask me to pull into a hotel parking lot so he could make some fundraising calls from a pay phone in the lobby (yes, children, there actually *was* a time before cell phones).

And woe to those whom Metzenbaum knew to be wealthy but who tried to poor-mouth their way out of contributing the amount he asked for.

Under federal campaign law, $2,000 was the most an individual could give to a campaign during an election cycle, meaning that married couples could give a total of $4,000—which Howard unfailingly asked for if he knew the person could afford it.

When one longtime donor sought to contribute less than the $4,000 maximum on the grounds that his business was having a bad year, Metzenbaum cut him off in midsentence.

"Tell you what," Howard said. "Don't send anything at all. You obviously need the money more than I do."

The donor's $4,000 check arrived a few days later.

But donors weren't the only ones whose feet Metzenbaum held to the fire.

Steaks and Bagels

He was at least equally tough on his campaign staff's expenditures—and often pored over expense reimbursement requests while we drove to various campaign events.

One time, during a campaign staff meeting at our headquarters in Cleveland, Howard waved a batch of expense reports over his head and volubly attacked what he regarded as the staff's profligate spending.

"My God," he thundered, "you people spend like a bunch of drunken sailors—and I can promise you it's going to stop right now."

Here, it should be pointed out that Metzenbaum's definition of "excessive" was itself rather expansive.

When I traveled alone on campaign business during the times the Senate was in session, I rarely ate lunch and frequently would stop for dinner on the road at a Ponderosa Steakhouse—a now nearly defunct national chain of bargain-basement "family" restaurants that dotted the national landscape during the 1970s and '80s.

One day, when reviewing my own expense reports, Howard turned to me and said in an exasperated tone, "I see that you eat at Ponderosa a lot—and that's fine. But do you always have to order the most expensive cuts?"

To this day, I have no idea if he was joking.

But I don't want to leave the impression that Howard was a curmudgeon who lacked a soft side.

He absolutely adored children and would frequently stop whatever he was doing to talk and even play with kids he met on the campaign trail.

One entire wall in his Senate office in Washington was reserved for "Metzenbabies"—a term he used to describe his staffers' children, whose photos he proudly displayed.

Once, when we stopped for me to pick something up at my home in Columbus, Howard donned a funny hat and cavorted on the staircase with two of my kids who were then ages five and three.

Later that year, when I called him at his Cleveland home a week or so after our Senate opponent George Voinovich began airing television ads implying that Howard was "soft on child pornography" (more on this later), Metzenbaum sounded noticeably depressed.

After talking with him for a moment or two about whatever it was I had called to discuss, I said, "Senator, you seem a little down in the dumps today. Is everything okay?"

"Oh, I'm fine," he said. "It's just that we all got home a few minutes ago from Temple where we were celebrating Rosh Hashanah. And when I turned the TV on for my grandkids, that damn child porn ad came on and they saw it. I really didn't know what to tell them."

Howard's religion, of course, was among the many ways in which he differed from both John Glenn and me.

Like John, I am of Scottish descent and have been a lifelong Presbyterian. Indeed, both Glenn and I were ordained elders in our church.

Metzenbaum, on the other hand, was a proudly practicing Jew—which sometimes led to amusing incidents.

After long days on the campaign trail, Howard and I would often spend the night at his home in Cleveland. On one occasion in late March, shortly after I joined the campaign and Metzenbaum's wife Shirley was still at their condo in Florida, Howard and I returned to the Cleveland house to sleep.

Arising early the next morning before the senator awakened, I discovered that the refrigerator was totally empty. Figuring I would get us breakfast, I consulted a phone book (they, too, were still a thing in the 1980s) and found a Jewish delicatessen not far away.

Being a longtime lover of lox and bagels, I got some for both of us and returned to Howard's house, where he was puttering around in the kitchen.

"Not to fear, Senator," I said while opening the bag and spreading our food out on the table, "I got us some breakfast."

Howard looked incredulous.

"What—you don't think Christians can like bagels, too?" I asked.

"I guess I knew some of you might like bagels," he said. "But I had no idea that *goys* knew anything about lox."

A Schott in the Dark

One of my favorite stories about Howard—mostly because it so well captures who he was—concerns April 4, opening day of the 1988 Major League Baseball season.

The Cincinnati Reds were playing a home game against the St. Louis Cardinals, one of their traditional rivals—and we in the campaign thought it a good idea for Metzenbaum to be in attendance.

The game was on a Monday.

Over the weekend, I got a telephone call from Charlie Luken, then the Democratic mayor of Cincinnati.

Luken told me he'd heard Howard was coming to the game and urged me to get him there an hour or so early so Metzenbaum could be part of the traditional March Across the Field that took place every opening day.

"It's great," Luken said. "Every elected officeholder who shows up—Democrat and Republican alike—lines up down the third base foul line and then we all walk across the field to show our support for the Reds, while the crowd cheers us. Howard should be part of it."

I thanked Luken for the heads-up, called Washington, and the staff booked Metzenbaum on an earlier flight so we wouldn't be late.

When I picked Howard up at the airport, he was decked out in a Reds jersey and was carrying—true story—a baseball glove. He evidently wanted to be fully prepared for any foul balls that came his way.

We drove to the stadium, and I escorted Metzenbaum down an aisle to a gate just to the left of the Reds dugout where a police officer was standing guard.

I could see all the other officeholders gathering near the left field foul line.

"This is Senator Metzenbaum," I told the guard, "and he's here to join the March Across the Field."

"OK, just a moment," the police officer said. "Let me tell Mrs. Schott."

Marge Schott was the Reds' owner, only the second woman to have owned an MLB team without having inherited it.

She was also very conservative in her politics and a large donor to GOP candidates and the Republican Party.

(Just *how* conservative Schott was would be revealed several years later when news broke that she had made anti-Semitic remarks and was a collector of Nazi memorabilia. The uproar was instantaneous and resulted in her being kicked out of Major League Baseball and forced to sell her ownership of the Reds—which landed her in one of Johnny Carson's *Tonight Show* monologues.

("There was good news and bad news for Cincinnati Reds owner Marge Schott this week," Carson said. "The bad news is that she was collecting Nazi paraphernalia and was forced to sell her ball club. But the good news is that she'll get a prime speaking spot at the next Republican National Convention.")

The police officer walked out to the pitching mound where Schott was standing with two of her omnipresent dogs and a small group of people.

After conferring with him for a moment, Schott looked at Howard and then sent the policeman back to us with a message.

"Mrs. Schott says that everyone who's supposed to be on the field is already *on* the field," he said.

"Wait a minute," I fumed. "What the hell is this? Senator Metzenbaum is an elected official, and *every* elected official is supposed to be welcome to march. I don't understand . . ."

Howard touched my arm. "It's okay," he said. "We'll just go to our seats."

Fortunately, I had sent out a press release that morning to all Cincinnati media telling them that Senator Metzenbaum would be at the game, giving them his seat number, and saying that he'd be available for interviews.

We did a lot of interviews that day, but Howard never mentioned Schott's disrespectful slighting of him. The Reds won the game in a thriller.

I've always presumed that Marge Schott was so pleased with herself that she couldn't resist telling people in the Reds front office how she had stuck it to Howard Metzenbaum.

And I've further presumed that her revelation was greeted with something along the lines of: "Are you out of your mind? Don't you realize that Howard Metzenbaum is chairman of the Senate's Antitrust Subcommittee—and that he's always threatening to jerk baseball's antitrust exemption?"

I presume these things because about a week after the incident, Metzenbaum opened a letter sent to him at his Senate office. Inside were two lifetime passes to all future home games of the Cincinnati Reds.

Further evidence that Marge Schott didn't know the measure of the man she'd insulted.

Howard simply tore the passes in half, put them in an envelope, and mailed them back to her. No note. No nothing. Just the shredded passes.

~

He's on *Our* Side

I've been involved in Ohio politics in one way or another since 1980.

I've either run or held senior positions in six different US Senate campaigns and been on the winning side in a majority of them.

But with the possible exception of Glenn's final reelection effort in 1992, Howard's 1988 campaign was the best I've ever been involved in.

The Metzenbaum campaign didn't make a single major mistake—and we capitalized on every one our opponents made.

Our in-house research operation was top notch, our pollster (Mark Mellman) was on the money, and our paid media firm (Doak & Shrum) was first rate.

We were, as they say, a well-oiled machine.

Both campaigns spent over $7 million apiece on that race—at the time, by far the most money spent on any political campaign in Ohio history. (To show how crazy and out-of-control things have gotten since, the 2024 Ohio Senate race between Sherrod Brown and Bernie Moreno racked up nearly *$500 million* in total spending.)

The '88 campaign was, at the beginning, the most-watched Senate race in the country—and one that virtually every pundit thought would be exceedingly close.

For those who may not be intimately familiar with Ohio geography, Interstate 70 cuts Ohio nearly in half, east to west.

In 1988, with the exception of some lightly populated rural areas, virtually everything north of I-70 was Democratic territory.

Virtually everything south—again with the exception of some lightly populated counties in southeast Ohio—was Republican.

George Voinovich was a moderate and the immensely popular mayor of Cleveland.

The GOP theory of the race was that Voinovich would cut deeply into Metzenbaum's support in the Cleveland media market, while racking up the usual Republican majorities in central (Columbus) and southwestern (Cincinnati) Ohio.

It wasn't a crazy theory—especially since Metzenbaum was, at that time, one of the most liberal members of either house of Congress. And Ohio was then a decidedly middle-of-the-road state.

But the Republican theory didn't take three things into account.

The first—which we saw in both our polling and focus groups—was that while Clevelanders liked having George Voinovich as their mayor, they also liked having Howard Metzenbaum as their senator.

And since Voinovich was "running from cover," they could keep Voinovich as their mayor and Metzenbaum as their senator simply by reelecting Howard.

That way, Metzenbaum would stay in the Senate—and Voinovich would stay in the mayor's office.

The second thing Republicans failed to adequately account for was Metzenbaum's populist image among the voters.

Sure, he may have been a liberal.

But he was also a fighter.

And as we also learned in our polling and focus groups, voters in 1988 simply didn't see "liberal" and "conservative" in the same way we do today—or the way political professionals did then.

In a 1987 focus group, for example, one voter told us he supported Metzenbaum for reelection because "he's a conservative like I am."

When asked what he meant by "conservative," the voter said, "Well, he stands up to the big oil companies and he doesn't take any s*** from the big utilities or drug companies. He stands up for people like me."

Perhaps you will not be surprised to learn that our 1988 campaign slogan became: "Metzenbaum: He's on *Our* Side."

Part of Howard's populist image was the result of his willingness—indeed, his fondness—for going toe to toe with both his friends (like organized labor) and his skeptics (like NRA members).

Over the course of that campaign, I watched Metzenbaum countless times chide union audiences for not doing enough, for taking his reelection for granted, and for (in his telling) their laziness and failure to have a sufficient sense of urgency.

Usually, this would come at the end of a speech as he climbed down from the podium, mic in hand, and waded into the crowd.

With his voice rising, Howard used his free hand to wave them up from their seats as he bellowed "Get up... I need your help... we're in the fight of our lives... it's time you GET OFF YOUR ASSES AND GET TO WORK."

Labor leaders are a proud bunch; few other politicians could get away with talking to them like that.

But with Howard, the theatrics never failed to achieve the desired result; his working-class audience would invariably rise as one, cheering, whistling, and giving the senator they knew to be "on their side" a thunderous standing ovation.

Even with voters less inclined to see him as an ally, Metzenbaum never hesitated to be similarly blunt.

In the western Ohio Republican stronghold of Lima, for example, Howard finished a campaign event at a local VFW hall where he spoke to a crowd of admirers.

Before leaving, however, he insisted on going downstairs to talk with the hall's bar patrons who hadn't come to the rally.

Most were friendly and readily shook his hand, with a few even asking for pictures with him.

At the end of the bar, though, two men sat sullenly, nursing their drinks.

Howard sauntered over and stuck out his hand. When they refused to take it, Metzenbaum asked them why.

"Because," one of them said, "we're members of the NRA—and you want to take away our guns."

"Move your asses over," Howard demanded, "I'm sitting down with you."

Though the men eyed him suspiciously, they complied and made room for the senator.

"Who told you I want to take away your guns?" he asked.

"We read it in the NRA magazine we get every month," one answered.

"Well, it's a damn lie," Howard said very matter-of-factly.

"I've got three bills pending in the Senate.

"One would require a three-day waiting period before you can buy a gun so the authorities can check to make sure you're not crazy or a convicted felon. You got a problem with that?"

Both men shook their heads no.

"My second bill requires that handguns made of plastic have a minimum amount of metal in them so they can't evade those metal detectors we have at airports. You got a problem with that one?"

The men looked at each other and both shook their heads again.

"And my third bill bans armor-piercing bullets that can penetrate those Kevlar vests police officers wear to protect themselves. Either of you have a problem with that?"

Both indicated they didn't.

"Well, that's it—those three bills are all the legislation I've got.

"And yet that NRA magazine makes me out to be some kind of antigun extremist. Just goes to show you can't believe everything you read, right?"

With that, Howard stuck out his hand again.

This time, both men shook it—and even smiled at him as they did so.

"Good talking with you fellows," Howard said. "Hope to have your votes in November."

I have no idea who those men ended up voting for.

But I wouldn't be surprised if they pulled the lever for Howard.

I'm absolutely certain they would have cast ballots for Voinovich had Metzenbaum not stopped to talk with them.

And at the very least, they now had a wonderful story to share with their friends and family members.

Chapter Eleven
The "Child Porn" Attack

THE THIRD THING REPUBLICANS DIDN'T take into account was the monumental gaffe Voinovich would commit in September when he accused Metzenbaum of being soft on child pornography.

The political fallout from that mistake was immense—and turned what likely would have been a close race into a fourteen-point Metzenbaum landslide on election day.

This was all the more remarkable because the Republican presidential candidate—George H. W. Bush—carried Ohio easily by eleven points that fall.

Indeed, 1988 marked the last time Ohio voters would split their tickets to favor Senate and presidential candidates from different parties running in a concurrent election.

So how did the high-risk (and, in the end, highly fatal) "child porn ad" come into being?

In our private polling—and likely in the polling of our opponent as well—Howard had held a modest but persistent lead from the outset and, by Labor Day, the Voinovich campaign evidently felt they had to try something dramatic in order to shake things up.

Moreover, George Voinovich was an inexperienced statewide candidate and was, in his own words, frustrated by his inability to make headway against Metzenbaum by focusing on traditional political issues.

Weeks after airing the TV ad that so badly boomeranged against him, Voinovich told *The Christian Science Monitor*:

> We have put out position paper after position paper on issues that are facing America. I have been with [newspaper] editorial boards who have never read them; some of them haven't even read the summary pieces. The very people who are telling me "You should run an issue-oriented campaign" don't even read the material we send them.... [Metzenbaum] is trying to fool people.... I really have to pierce that veil and really get people to understand who he is and what he stands for.

To do that, the Voinovich campaign recruited a "concerned Ohio mother" (who, in reality, turned out to be a relative of one of his campaign operatives) to look into a camera lens and declare:

> He votes against laws that will put child pornographers out of business. I want to put Howard Metzenbaum out of business.

From today's vantage point—when voters have become inured to far more vicious political attacks—it's probably hard to fathom how shocking the Voinovich ad was in 1988, not only because of the subject matter but also because voters had not yet become comfortable with this level of personal assault.

And we who led the Metzenbaum campaign immediately realized that the ad could pose an existential threat to his reelection and required a quick response.

We knew that if voters came to actually *believe* the charge, Howard might not survive.

Here, permit me to circle back to my appearances on the game show *Jeopardy!* that I mentioned earlier.

On the first day Voinovich's "child porn" ad aired on TV, a frantic woman viewer called Ohio Democratic Party headquarters to sound the alarm—and was routed to Lynn Plannick, then the ODP's executive director.

The caller was in full panic mode, calling the ad "terrible" and imploring the party to "do something."

Plannick assured the woman that the Metzenbaum campaign was aware of the ad and that our "communications director" (by which she meant me) was on top of it.

"But you don't understand," the woman told Lynn, "this ad is truly horrible and if it takes hold, there's no way Howard will be able to recover."

Plannick again tried to reassure her. "I appreciate your concern, ma'am, but Howard has a first-rate communications director and I'm absolutely confident he'll come up with an effective response and that everything will be okay."

With that, Lynn told me, there was a long pause on the other end of the phone line.

Finally, the woman said, "What's this communication guy's name?"

"Dale Butland," Plannick replied.

Another pause.

"Oh yeah? Well, he didn't do so goddamn good on *Jeopardy!*, did he?"

~

Fighting Back

As Metzenbaum's communications director, I was, as previously mentioned, headquartered in Columbus, where I worked out of an office rented from the ODP.

After a round of emergency telephone calls back to Washington with Peter Harris, our campaign consultants, and the senator himself, everyone agreed time was of the essence and that we had to work fast.

Our research team quickly looked into the legislation on which the Voinovich campaign based its attack.

As is usually the case in situations like this, the provisions dealing with child pornography were contained in an amendment to a much larger bill that raised a host of constitutional issues with which Metzenbaum had been concerned.

Moreover—and this was important—Metzenbaum had actually ended up *supporting* the bill that contained the anti–child porn amendment.

Having gathered the facts, we were now ready to swing into action.

My first call was to Senator Glenn.

I filled him in on both the ad and the legislation used to justify it, and told him Howard would be calling to ask that he appear in a response ad that our paid media team was already writing.

Glenn immediately agreed to come to Howard's defense.

The Voinovich ad first ran on a Tuesday, the day after Labor Day.

By Thursday morning, John was meeting with our media team in Washington to film his response.

As noted earlier, in 1988, there were no cellphones, desk and laptop computers were still in their infancy, and digital communication was not yet in widespread use.

What passed for high tech in those days were "fax machines," which could transmit copies (or facsimiles) of documents over telephone lines.

By Friday, I was laboriously sending faxes to every Ohio print and electronic media political reporter . . . to every newspaper editorial board . . . and to every major television and radio commentator in the state.

The documents I sent included the text of the Voinovich ad, an analysis of the legislation on which it was based, pages from the *Congressional Record* showing that Howard had, in fact, voted for the legislation that included the child pornography amendment, and "talking points" explaining why the Voinovich attack was not only false but ugly and contemptuous to boot.

For the next week, I worked sixteen-hour days sending the material and fielding calls from those to whom I sent it, answering their questions and explaining why what Voinovich had intimated was far beyond the pale of what should be acceptable political discourse.

Here, it's probably worth noting for younger readers—or maybe any reader who has forgotten what politics were like before Donald Trump—that in the "old days," it was usually game over for any politician who got caught in a lie.

Today, we live in an essentially post-truth era where politics have become so thoroughly tribalized that facts no longer matter to large swaths of the electorate.

Despite fact-checkers catching him in over *thirty thousand* lies during his first term as president (and despite his continued adherence to the Big Lie that the 2020 presidential election was "rigged" and "stolen" from him), Donald Trump won the presidency again in 2024—and this time, by a more comfortable margin than he had the first time around.

The political atmosphere in 1988 was, to say the least, very different. Politicians—and those who worked for them—lived in mortal fear of the media catching them in an untruth.

Statistics cited in press releases or TV ads were double- and triple-checked for accuracy.

Attacks on one's electoral opponent, especially in high-profile contests, were even more carefully scrutinized for accuracy.

For their part, voters generally relied on the judgments and verdicts rendered by newspaper columnists and television anchors whom they viewed as honest brokers.

If these "enforcers" concluded that a charge or allegation was false, misleading, or below the belt, voters routinely made offenders pay at the ballot box.

It was a different—and better—world.

~

Meanwhile, as I was beavering away on the fax machines, Glenn's response ad was airing on every television station in Ohio.

As was often true when he felt strongly about something, Glenn had added—and in some cases, substituted—his own words in the script he'd been given.

Voinovich's cheap-shot attack, Glenn intoned, "is the worst gutter politics I've seen in a long time. And this ad says a lot more about George Voinovich than it does about Howard Metzenbaum."

Though John had his challenges when it came to speechmaking, no politician I ever worked with was better at "candidate-to-camera" TV ads than Glenn—who also had a preternatural ability to time his words perfectly to the seconds he was allotted.

(For a 30-second TV spot, the content typically can go no longer than 26 or 27 seconds, leaving the remaining 3–4 seconds for the voice-over "disclaimer" telling viewers who approved and paid for the ad to air. If ad-makers told Glenn they "needed 26 seconds" from him, John would uncannily give them precisely 26 seconds; I was never able to discern exactly how he did it).

John's ad defending Metzenbaum was an absolute game changer. It was not only compelling, coming from a national hero, but authentically conveyed the outrage Glenn genuinely felt.

Both campaigns put enormous amounts of money into airing these dueling TV ads; Voinovich, in fact, actually doubled down on his vile accusation with two *more* ads that expanded the charges against Howard.

Some television stations, whether intentionally or coincidentally, ran the ads back-to-back, with Voinovich's attack running first and John's response following immediately after. Getting "the last word" obviously worked in our favor.

Before long, Ohio's newspaper editorial boards and TV commentariat were weighing in with a virtually unanimous verdict: Voinovich had badly overstepped with an ugly smear that was wholly unjustified.

As the *Cleveland Plain Dealer* put it: "it looks for all the world like a desperation move by a candidate down in the polls."

One of the most lethal Voinovich takedowns was offered by longtime Cleveland newspaper columnist Dick Feagler, who had gone to school with Voinovich, counted him as a friend, and whose popular Saturday night television show had an enormous audience across much of northeast Ohio.

"We've known each other for a long time," Feagler said, "and this isn't the George Voinovich I know."

The "child porn" furor lasted two weeks.

I furiously faxed every editorial or op-ed that was critical of Voinovich's ad to the entire Ohio press corps, as well as to every daily newspaper that had not yet publicly commented on the affair.

By the end of September, the battle was over—and the Senate race was, too.

Howard Metzenbaum was going to win; the only question was by how much.

In his landslide win on election day, Howard carried not just Democratic strongholds like Cleveland, Toledo, Youngstown, and Dayton, but Republican cities like Columbus and Cincinnati, too.

In fact, the senator's victory was so complete that he won every single ward in the city of Cleveland including, embarrassingly for Republicans, even Mayor Voinovich's home neighborhood of Collinwood.

Chapter Twelve

Redemption

Glenn's Speech to the 1988 Democratic National Convention

TWO MONTHS BEFORE THE ELECTION-DEFINING child porn ad that would cement Senator Metzenbaum's win, the 1988 Democratic National Convention met in Atlanta to nominate Massachusetts Governor Michael Dukakis for president.

Since Dukakis's nomination was wrapped up relatively early in the primary season, the only drama leading up to the convention was who he would tap to be his vice-presidential running mate.

Glenn—who had been reelected to a third Senate term just two years earlier in the nation's most important swing state—was an early favorite among pundits and was thoroughly vetted by the Dukakis campaign.

In the end, Dukakis chose Texas Senator Lloyd Bentsen and John once again was left standing at the altar.

Less than a week before the convention kicked off on July 18, Bentsen called to ask if John would introduce him when he accepted the VP nomination.

Glenn readily assented, then phoned me to say I needed to write the speech.

Since John's introduction—like Bentsen's acceptance—would be televised to a national audience, we both knew the stakes were enormous.

It was, after all, the first time Glenn would speak to a Democratic National Convention since his disastrous keynote address in 1976.

After hearing from John, my first calls were to Metzenbaum and his campaign manager Peter Harris, who immediately granted me a week-and-a-half leave of absence from the Senate campaign so I could write the speech and then travel with Glenn to Atlanta, where Howard would himself be a convention delegate from Ohio.

Because television coverage is vital to presidential candidates, everything at a convention is carefully choreographed and tightly scripted.

Convention speeches are timed to the nanosecond, drafts must be approved days in advance by the presidential nominee's staff—and, at the '88 convention, speakers were required to participate in a "dress rehearsal" the day before taking the stage.

A replica of the speakers' rostrum—smaller, but otherwise identical to the one that would be used on the convention floor—was constructed underneath the Omni arena in Atlanta.

Stopwatches were used to time rehearsals and ensure that no one's remarks would go longer than the time allotted.

Though at first blush this might seem extreme, the reasoning behind it makes perfect sense. No party can afford to have long-winded warm-up speakers delay the speeches of its nominees past prime-time TV hours.

This, in fact, disastrously happened in 1972 when the fractious Democratic National Convention produced so many speakers and internecine fights that the party's presidential nominee—George McGovern—didn't take the stage until 3:00 a.m. Eastern Time, long after most of the national audience had gone to bed.

In any event, Dukakis's campaign team informed us that John's nominating speech for Bentsen could not exceed ten minutes.

And that, I knew, necessitated what might be called a "bumper sticker" speech; one that was short on exposition but long on applause lines that would give delegates a generous serving of partisan red meat.

Because John had been the featured speaker at a passel of state and county Democratic Party dinners before I went to work for the Metzenbaum campaign, we already had a number of good applause lines in our back pocket that we knew would work.

The mission, I decided, was to take the best of those, come up with some new ones that were convention-specific, and then tie them together with a few appropriate transitions in between.

One particular target I knew we wanted to hit was the Religious Right, which in 1988 was riding high with Jerry Falwell touting his "Moral Majority" and televangelists like Jim Bakker and Jimmy Swaggert weeping their way across television screens from one end of America to the other as they collected money, championed Republicans, and condemned Democrats.

Given his patriotic, clean-cut, all-American image, John was uniquely positioned to take on these cleric-politicians masquerading as pastors—along with Reagan administration cheerleaders like Attorney General Ed Meese who were egging them on.

But we only had ten minutes.

And as Winston Churchill once observed, writing a short speech is far more difficult and time-consuming than writing a long one.

Ten minutes leaves no room for wasted words; *every* word must count.

It is a speechwriting axiom that an oration's opening lines are crucial; you only get one chance to "hook" your audience.

And nowhere is that truer than at a rowdy political convention where delegates, party guests, and the media covering the show are easily distracted and often decide in the opening moments whether the person on the dais is worth listening to.

Figuring out how to open Glenn's speech was further complicated by the fact that everyone in the audience would know that John himself had been considered as Dukakis's vice-presidential running mate but had ultimately been rejected.

Was Glenn miffed at being spurned?

How would he handle the awkwardness of introducing the man who had beaten him out?

If you've read this far, you know that I've always believed humor is an undervalued political tool.

Even (or, perhaps, especially) when you're eviscerating an opponent, the attack almost always goes down better if it's leavened with humor. And the chances of winning an election are greatly enhanced if a politician can get voters laughing at his or her opponent.

All of which was why I decided that humor—including a bit of self-deprecating humor—was the best way for Glenn to break the ice, deal with the awkwardness of introducing the man who had nosed him out for VP, and capture the audience right out of the gate.

When he was introduced—and after the cheering, whistling, and foot stomping coming from the Ohio delegation subsided—Glenn waited a beat or two... looked out at the assembled Democrats... shook his head slightly and said:

"I just *knew* I'd be making a speech tonight about the vice presidency."

Whatever tension there had been immediately dissipated. The convention crowd laughed, clapped, and roared their approval.

John never took his foot off the gas.

He turned next to the comparative Texas bona fides of Senator Lloyd Bentsen—the man he was introducing—and those of the incumbent vice president, George H. W. Bush, who was now the Republican nominee for president.

Bush claimed a Texas residency despite growing up as a Connecticut Yankee who spent his summers at the hoity-toity Bush family compound on the coast of Maine.

Bush was also widely perceived as prissy, patrician, and, let's be honest, the very embodiment of country club elitism.

"To get to the Senate in 1970, Lloyd Bentsen beat George Bush," Glenn began. "And that's because Texas voters know a REAL Texan when they see one."

"Now we all know that George Bush *says* he's a real Texan, too.

"But let me ask you this question:

"How many *real* Texans do *you* know whose idea of Mexican food is refried quiche?"

The convention audience erupted in laughter, cheers, and applause.

"And there are other differences too.... Lloyd Bentsen knows that on economics, Ronald Reagan and George Bush have it backwards. *True* prosperity always flows *up* from the people and never trickles *down* from the powerful.

"The White House says there's nothing we can do about unfair foreign trade that closes American factories and steals American jobs.

"Well, Lloyd Bentsen believes that when other countries take advantage of us, you can't talk like Rambo and act like Bambi.

"And when it comes to women's rights, George Bush is part of an administration that consistently takes its cues from right-wing zealots.

"They gloated about the defeat of the ERA, and then boasted about appointing the first woman to the U.S. Supreme Court.

"But Lloyd Bentsen knows there is a huge difference between making one woman a Justice—and bringing justice to American women.

"And let me say that I'm also tired of right-wing *religious* extremism—and of those who believe that they—and only they—know and hold the truth.

"We Democrats cherish our churches and we treasure our faiths.

"I'm proud to say I've been an Elder in the Presbyterian Church for over twenty-five years, and I'll tell you what *I* believe.

"I believe the last thing this country needs is to have the Gospels of Matthew, Mark, Luke, and John rewritten by Meese, Bakker, Swaggert, and Falwell."

The Convention Hall repeatedly exploded in cheers and chants of "Go, John, Go."

"Our opponents also talk about 'law and order'—and about how George Bush will be tough on crime.

"But in this administration, over one hundred officials have already been indicted or left office under an ethical cloud.

"And yet despite that record, they tell us they want 'Four More Years.'

"But at the rate they're going, I think some of them are going to end up serving ten to twenty."

And so it went, with applause line after applause line inspiring multiple standing ovations, as well as that staple of all national political conventions, a few "spontaneous demonstrations."

The unanticipated interruptions stretched Glenn's ten-minute text into a twenty-two-minute stem-winder.

It was among the best-received speeches at the '88 convention and, more importantly for John, finally buried the "dull and boring" image that had shadowed him for over a decade.

For speechwriters, who generally labor in anonymity, there is no sweeter reward than having your boss do well on a national stage.

At a reception for the Ohio convention contingent later that night, John was warmly embraced by Buckeye delegates who bathed him in heartfelt congratulations. He had made them proud. One of the first to hug John and heartily shake his hand was his Senate colleague, Howard Metzenbaum.

The media's reaction was equally positive, with the sentiment of the Ohio press corps probably best summed up by Steve Luttner of the *Cleveland Plain Dealer,* who left a two-word message for me at my hotel: "Home Run."

The next day, I flew home to Ohio to resume my work for the Metzenbaum campaign.

Four months later, Howard's landslide win would send him back to Washington.

For me, the best and longest-lasting reward I received for working on the Metzenbaum campaign was meeting an executive assistant to Ohio Governor Richard Celeste; a beautiful, warm, witty, creative, and classy woman who, five years later, would become my wife and an amazing parent to the five children in our blended family.

On March 13, 2025, Vicki and I celebrated our thirty-second wedding anniversary.

She is the love of my life.

Chapter Thirteen

The Keating Five Investigation and Hearings

FOLLOWING THE CAMPAIGN AND A short, postelection vacation in Florida, I returned to Glenn's Senate office in mid-November, ready to face whatever challenges lay ahead for us in the remaining years of John's third term.

As it turned out, those years would be eventful.

In a bad way.

They were the Keating Five years.

As mentioned earlier, the "Keating Five" senators—four Democrats and one Republican—had met with federal investigators in 1987 at the urging of Charles Keating, a one-time Ohio businessman and erstwhile anti-pornography crusader who was suspected of violating a number of federal investment rules.

Keating complained that the investigation had gone on too long and was casting a cloud over his Lincoln Savings & Loan business.

All he wanted, Keating said, was "fairness"; specifically, that regulators either charge him with a crime or bring their investigation to a close.

When the senators' meetings with government investigators became public (Glenn attended only one; the other four senators attended several), the Senate Ethics Committee launched a full-blown investigation of its own in November 1989, hiring Washington superlawyer Robert Bennett as special counsel.

Bennett's investigation lasted nine months, following which he submitted his findings, along with a recommendation that the Ethics Committee conduct public hearings.

Those findings were contained in a confidential report given to the Ethics Committee on September 10, 1990—which, unsurprisingly, was quickly leaked to the news media.

Bennett's key recommendation was that the committee continue its investigation into the conduct of Senators Cranston, DeConcini, and Riegle, but that Glenn and Arizona Senator John McCain be cut loose because investigators had found no evidence of wrongdoing on their parts.

Ah, but this was Washington—a place where politics *always* reigns supreme.

The Senate and House Ethics Committees are unique in that they are the only ones in Congress with an equal number of Republicans and Democrats.

On all other committees, the party controlling the chamber (that is, the "majority party") has at least one more member than the minority party, thus obviating the possibility of a tie should all committee members vote along party lines on whatever matter is at issue.

The Senate committee was composed of three Democratic senators and three Republicans—with Democrat Howell Heflin of Alabama and Republican Warren Rudman of New Hampshire serving as cochairmen.

Though the leak of Bennett's confidential report occurred almost immediately after it was submitted, weeks of inaction followed as Democratic and Republican committee members discussed his findings and recommendations separately and in secret.

Glenn naturally assumed the committee would follow the lead of its own special counsel and felt confident that his days in the investigative dock would soon be over.

And that would certainly be welcome news from a financial perspective.

Glenn—like his colleagues—had hired a high-priced Washington attorney to help him navigate the investigatory process.

And the legal eagle he'd hired—Charles ("Chuck") Ruff, who had been a chief Watergate prosecutor and a former US attorney—didn't come cheap.

Glenn had already spent over $100,000 in legal fees out of his own pocket.

When no word or action from the committee was forthcoming, John grew frustrated by the seemingly inexplicable holdup.

And when the committee finally announced—on October 23—that it was rejecting Bennett's recommendation and would keep both "Johns" (McCain and Glenn) in the investigation, he was both angry and bewildered.

It wasn't until weeks later that he finally learned what had happened from Warren Rudman—ironically, the *Republican* cochair of the committee.

And the truth was painful.

John had been betrayed by a fellow *Democrat*; the other committee cochair, Howell Heflin of Alabama.

Because four of the five senators involved with the Keating matter were Democrats, Heflin feared that dropping Glenn and McCain (the only Republican) would make the matter an "all-Democrat scandal."

He therefore feverishly lobbied his two Democratic committee colleagues to keep Glenn in the mix since it was the only way they could keep McCain in.

The committee vote was 3–3, with all Republicans voting to dismiss Glenn and McCain as Bennett had recommended—and all Democrats rejecting that recommendation.

In the absence of a majority, the special counsel's recommendation was not agreed to.

To say Glenn was furious with Heflin would be a vast understatement.

Nothing was more important to John than his good name and lifelong reputation for integrity.

Not only was he embarrassed by the whole affair (describing the Keating situation to me as "one of the lowest points in my life"), but now he would endure the further humiliation of being included in nationally televised hearings for no other reason than pure politics.

To my knowledge, he never spoke to Heflin again for the rest of their years in the Senate.

The hearings were held in the Hart Senate Office Building (where Glenn's own office was located) and lasted seven weeks, from November 15, 1990, to January 16, 1991.

In the end, the committee found that Glenn's involvement in the Keating scheme had been minimal and voted to drop the charges against him.

He was criticized only for exercising "poor judgment" in setting up a later meeting between Keating and then–House Speaker Jim Wright.

The committee's action came as close to an exoneration of Glenn as was politically possible—but it was a costly one, nevertheless.

For the first and only time in his life, John's honesty and character had been called into question.

And by the time the hearings were over, he had spent well over $250,000 of his own money in legal fees.

But the Keating Five affair did have one salutary outcome.

Before the hearings, John was wrestling with the question of whether or not to seek another term in the Senate. By the time it was over, that question had been fully answered.

Glenn would seek vindication from the voters in 1992.

He was now dead set on running, winning, and becoming the first and only four-term elected senator in Ohio history.

Chapter Fourteen

The 1992 Reelection Campaign, Part I

IT PROBABLY HAS NOT ESCAPED notice that I've given relatively short shrift to Glenn's 1980 and 1986 reelection campaigns. That's partly because the outcome of those races was never in doubt and partly because the campaigns themselves were not particularly interesting.

The 1992 reelection effort, however, was different.

Not only would it prove to be John's last campaign, it would also be his most difficult.

His orbital flight was now thirty years in the past, and a substantial portion of the Ohio electorate had no living memory of it.

For them, John Glenn was a name in a history book, not an unassailable national hero who transcended partisan politics.

He also had now run for president and amassed an eighteen-year congressional voting record, both of which clearly established him as a Democrat.

And Ohio was changing politically.

In the early 1980s, Democrats had been the state's dominant party, holding every statewide office, both houses of the state legislature, the

Ohio Supreme Court, both US Senate seats, and a majority in the state's congressional delegation.

But Republicans were beginning to reassert themselves.

They took control of the Ohio Senate in 1985.

They elected a chief justice of the Ohio Supreme Court in 1986.

And in 1990—just two years after losing a Senate race to Howard Metzenbaum in a landslide—George Voinovich was elected governor. The same year, Republicans also defeated a young, Democratic *wunderkind* named Sherrod Brown who was running for reelection as Ohio secretary of state.

In addition, Glenn was haunted by the gnawing debt left over from his 1984 presidential campaign, and the Keating Five affair had further tarnished his previously pristine image.

For all these reasons, John's 1992 campaign was unlikely to be a slam dunk.

And, indeed, it was not.

Few people outside the upper echelon of our campaign know how close John came to losing.

Explaining why will require a road trip into the campaign's strategies, personalities, inner workings, twists, turns, and key moments.

I believe the ride will prove worthwhile.

Let me start with my own role.

Though I had held senior positions in three previous US Senate campaigns (Glenn's in both 1980 and '86, and Metzenbaum's in 1988), I had never been fully in charge of one.

I was, therefore, a bit taken aback when in the early months of 1991, John asked if I would run his 1992 reelection effort.

That I was now living in Columbus rather than Washington wasn't a problem; Glenn had always felt strongly that his campaigns should be headquartered in Ohio anyway.

He also instinctively knew that 1992 was likely to be the toughest campaign of his career.

He was well aware that Republicans thought the Keating Five fiasco, coupled with John's leftover presidential campaign debt, had not only weakened him politically, but punctured his aura of electoral invincibility.

Nevertheless, he still hoped (naively, in my view) that the campaign would somehow be entirely positive and upbeat, devoid of personal attacks and political mudslinging.

Burned by the "hired guns" who had guided his presidential run, Glenn told me he wanted to put someone in charge of this one whom he trusted implicitly and whose loyalties he need never doubt.

I unhesitatingly accepted the position and immediately turned my attention to building a campaign team that I thought would be up to the challenge.

Who should do our polling was the easiest call.

The late Mark Mellman had not only polled for Glenn in 1986 and Metzenbaum in 1988 but was, by 1992, perhaps the most celebrated Democratic pollster in Washington. An extra bonus was that Mark was a native Ohioan, having grown up in the Columbus suburb of Bexley.

Rehiring him was a total no-brainer.

I also knew that I would need a deputy I could trust and who possessed some of the administrative skills I lacked.

From at least the time of the Delphic Oracle, "know thyself" has been good advice.

It's important to know your strengths. But it's at least equally important to know your weaknesses—and to be willing to compensate for them.

Organization charts, accounting and budgetary spreadsheets, volunteer management, and even such mundane tasks as purchasing yard signs and campaign buttons require administrative skills that simply are not in my wheelhouse.

But through my time with the Metzenbaum campaign, I had come to know someone who *did* have those skills.

So while I assumed the title of campaign director, I hired Metzenbaum staffer Kevin Bruns to be our day-to-day campaign manager.

While I (and, when necessary, the senator himself) would approve all major decisions, Kevin's job was to ensure our campaign train ran smoothly and on time.

My most difficult decision—or, more precisely, the decision I knew would be the most difficult sell—was who our paid media consultant would be.

For the uninitiated, "paid media" is what regular people call "TV and radio advertising."

It is distinct from news coverage, which is known as "free" or "earned" media.

In 1992—before the advent of digital communication and social media—advertising on television and, to a lesser extent, radio was pretty much the whole ballgame.

Billboards and even newspaper ads had largely gone the way of the dodo.

Newspaper editorial endorsements remained important—but mostly because they could be touted in thirty-second television spots, since broadcast TV and the emergent cable networks had become the primary sources of information for most Americans.

For political campaigns, television ads had another enormous advantage over newspaper ads.

Newspapers are an "active" medium, meaning that in order to receive the message, the voter has to take the affirmative step of actually *reading* the ad.

Television, by contrast, is a "passive" medium, meaning that the voter need not do anything to get the message.

In fact, viewers *will* get the message unless they take an active step *not* to get it by, say, turning the TV off, changing the station, getting something to eat, or going to the bathroom.

It probably will come as no surprise that a huge amount of research had been done regarding how often someone has to see a message on TV before it's remembered (or "burned in," as those in the business sometimes said).

While the rule of thumb may have changed over the intervening years, in 1992 it was generally thought that a political "message" had to be seen by a viewer at least seven times to be burned in.

This number was vitally important since it determined how often an ad had to air in order to be effective.

And that, in turn, determined how much money a campaign had to spend on it.

At the risk of descending a bit into the weeds, how often a TV ad airs is determined by how many "gross ratings points"—or GRPs—are put behind it.

One thousand gross ratings points means that the average viewer will see the ad once.

At a minimum, then, campaigns had to buy at least seven thousand gross ratings points for a particular ad to do the job, and ten thousand GRPs was even more effective.

How much a campaign pays per GRP varies according to the size of the media market.

A larger market—like Cleveland or Columbus—will cost more per gross ratings point because ads airing in larger markets obviously will be seen by more viewers than ads run in smaller markets.

Most states only have one, two, or three television media markets, typically located in their (few) big cities.

But Ohio has a comparatively *large* number of major cities (and, therefore, TV media markets): Cleveland, Columbus, Cincinnati, Toledo, Dayton, Youngstown, and two West Virginia cities (Wheeling and Huntington) whose stations serve viewers in the eastern part of our state along the Ohio River.

And that wasn't all.

In 1992, Lima—in the western part of the state—had a couple of network-affiliated stations, and Zanesville—in east-central Ohio—had one, making them the ninth and tenth TV media markets in the state.

Akron and Canton were Ohio's other large cities, but did not constitute their own media markets since their residents watched Cleveland television.

In short, Ohio was one of the more expensive states in the nation for paid media campaigns.

One intriguing aside: New Jersey—which didn't have a single network-affiliated television station within its borders—was at that time the *most expensive* state in which to run a media campaign.

Why?

Because northern New Jersey residents watched New York City television stations, while those in the southern part of the state got their TV from Philadelphia, two of the costliest media markets in the nation.

And that was a pity for New Jersey candidates running for statewide offices like governor or the US Senate: They paid a boatload of money to air ads that would reach millions upon millions of viewers, only a fraction of whom could actually vote in New Jersey.

In any event, television advertising in politics was king, the lion's share of any statewide campaign was devoted to it, and the effectiveness of a campaign's TV ads was often the difference between victory and defeat in closely contested elections.

~

The Media Consultant Battle

I knew which media firm I wanted to hire for John's reelection campaign.

At the time, the Washington-based firm of Doak & Shrum (later, Doak, Shrum and Associates) was among the hottest Democratic media operations in the nation.

Among other victories, they had helped elect governors in Mississippi and Pennsylvania, mayors in Denver, Philadelphia, and San Francisco, and US senators in Maryland, California, and, of course, Ohio.

The principals were David Doak—a Missouri lawyer I didn't know well who had been a prosecuting attorney before getting into politics—and Bob Shrum, Senator Edward Kennedy's former press secretary and speechwriter who, as I mentioned earlier, had been a friend since we first met in the early 1980s.

Most significantly, Doak & Shrum had Ohio experience, since they had done the paid media for Metzenbaum's 1988 reelection campaign—and their work was superb.

Another huge plus was that Peter Harris—Metzenbaum's campaign manager, with whom I had become close—had recently joined the firm and would be a key part of their effort on behalf of Glenn.

Still, I knew Doak & Shrum would be a hard sell and would almost certainly get pushback from both Glenn and his administrative assistant—Mary Jane Veno—but for very different reasons.

For John, hiring Doak & Shrum would mean casting aside Bill Connell, whose one-man media shop had produced the television ads for John's 1980 and 1986 campaigns.

I liked Bill personally but felt his ads were of the bland, cookie-cutter variety that would be insufficient for the kind of bare-knuckled campaign into which I was sure we were headed.

In 1992, I felt, positive ads that simply built John up would not be enough.

We would also need hard-edged, take-no-prisoners attack ads capable of bringing our opponent down.

And Bill Connell was not that kind of ad-maker.

For Mary Jane Veno, who had improbably worked her way up from being Glenn's scheduler to serving as his Washington chief of staff, loyalty to Bill Connell wasn't the issue.

Though she shared my view about Connell's unsuitability for the upcoming campaign, Veno was extremely close to Paul Tipps, a former chairman of the Ohio Democratic Party who had become one of the state's most successful and influential lobbyists.

And Tipps, I strongly suspected, would be pushing hard for his friend, Gerald ("Jerry") Austin, to do Glenn's paid media.

I didn't know Austin well at the time, but had enormous respect for his talent.

A Bronx-born Ohio transplant, Jerry had served as chief political strategist for former Ohio Governor Richard Celeste and guided his campaigns to victory in both 1982 and 1986.

He then built a national reputation by, among other things, being the architect of Carol Moseley Braun's astonishing US Senate win in Illinois, and then serving as the Reverend Jesse Jackson's 1988 presidential campaign manager.

Moreover, Austin was everything Connell wasn't: brash, irreverent, and capable of creating the kind of clever, smash-mouth TV ads that I believed would be needed in our upcoming campaign.

In truth, I greatly admired Jerry years before I met him.

In May 1970—the same month and year I graduated from college in Texas—Ohio Republican Governor James Rhodes tried to quell anti–Vietnam War protests at Kent State University by sending National Guard troops onto the campus.

The result—four students shot to death by the Guard—literally changed my career path.

Before Kent State, I had been an undergraduate psychology major intent on pursuing a postgraduate degree in clinical psychology.

After Kent State, I decided to shift academic gears and study government and political science in graduate school.

In 1986, Rhodes, who had served four previous terms as governor, was attempting to make a political comeback.

But his decades-long political career came to an abrupt and final end when Democrat Dick Celeste overwhelmingly defeated him in a bruising reelection campaign that Austin managed.

When Jerry was asked on election night to comment on Rhodes's defeat, he said, "Four Ohio kids are sleeping better in Heaven tonight knowing that son of a bitch will never be governor again."

I wanted to stand up and cheer.

Still, six years later, I did not believe Jerry was our best choice in 1992. Partly because he—like Connell—was, at least creatively, a one-man show.

While Austin's ads were often brilliant, so too were those of Doak & Shrum.

The difference was that with Jerry, we'd get one creative mind.

With Doak & Shrum, we'd get several: Doak, Shrum, Peter Harris, and Tad Devine (who years later would do the paid media for Bernie Sanders's 2020 presidential campaign).

If two heads are better than one, I reasoned, four would be better yet.

Plus, Doak & Shrum, unlike Austin, had recently helped elect a US senator in Ohio.

The battle lines thus were drawn, with me whispering "Doak & Shrum" in one of Glenn's ears, while Tipps and Veno whispered "Jerry Austin" in the other.

To resolve the dispute, Glenn decided on a meeting where Tipps and I would make our respective cases.

Only top Senate staffers were invited to sit in, along with John's wife and lifelong partner, Annie.

The meeting took place in early spring and the atmosphere was tense.

Tipps spoke first and pitched Austin; I followed with an appeal for Doak & Shrum.

A discussion ensued, in which Glenn asked a host of questions including, of course, how much money each of the consultants would charge for their services.

Things became heated only after Tipps felt the need to attack Doak, Shrum, and Peter Harris in personal terms, which I considered both unprofessional and uncalled for.

Glenn halted the hostilities and brought the meeting to a close by thanking Tipps and me for our presentations and saying, as was his custom, that he wanted to think the matter over before making a final decision.

Two days later, we had an answer.

Doak & Shrum would be our media firm.

Paul Tipps, who was not used to losing, held a grudge against me for years afterward.

Though Austin was naturally disappointed, we stayed in touch and have worked together on many different Democratic projects and initiatives over the years.

I respect him immensely and consider him a dear friend.

Chapter Fifteen
The 1992 Reelection Campaign, Part II

FOR THEIR PART, OHIO REPUBLICANS chose Mike DeWine as their party's Senate standard-bearer.

An attorney and scion of a wealthy family who owned a seed business, DeWine began his political career as a prosecutor in Greene County (near Dayton), then served one term in the Ohio Senate before successfully running for a west-central Ohio congressional seat he held for eight years.

Rather than run for reelection to Congress in 1990, DeWine joined the GOP gubernatorial ticket and became George Voinovich's running mate, thus landing himself the job of lieutenant governor, the office he held at the time he challenged Glenn two years later.

Though possessed of a bland personality that teeters on the edge of nerdy and oozes whatever the opposite of charisma is, DeWine's post-1992 political career has been nothing short of dazzling: two-term US Senator, two-term state attorney general, and two terms as governor of Ohio.

Although DeWine was hardly a household political name in 1992, state and national Republicans smelled blood, and we knew raising money would not pose a problem for him.

Nor did he have any trouble attracting some top campaign talent.

DeWine's campaign manager was Curt Steiner, an up-and-coming political strategist who managed Voinovich's winning gubernatorial campaign in 1990, and has gone on to become one of the most successful GOP operatives in modern Ohio history.

DeWine's polling was done by the Washington-based Tarrance Group, a highly respected GOP firm, and paid media was handled by a brilliant young phenomenon named Greg Stevens, who years later would tragically pass away from cancer at the age of fifty-eight.

With talented teams for both candidates now in place, my job as campaign director got off to an inauspicious start.

In the spring—while I was still serving as Glenn's Senate press secretary—our campaign researchers uncovered evidence that one of DeWine's donors had also made several contributions to David Duke, a former Grand Wizard of the Ku Klux Klan who had run unsuccessfully as the Republican candidate for Louisiana governor in 1991.

Thinking it an interesting tidbit, I passed the information on to an Ohio newspaper reporter.

Whereupon it promptly blew up in my face.

Rather than the reporter's story being about DeWine and Duke having a common contributor, the thrust of his piece was that I was playing dirty pool right out of the gate and that the coming campaign was sure to be ugly and negative.

For the first and only time in all the years I worked for him, Glenn was absolutely furious with me.

He was still laboring under the illusion that the '92 campaign might be a mild and gentlemanly affair in which he and his opponent would stick to "the issues" and refrain from attacking one another personally.

And now I had fired the first shot in a war he had hoped to avoid.

After dressing me down in no uncertain terms, John ordered me to immediately put out a statement that made his displeasure clear.

I did—and then sheepishly confirmed to any journalist who asked that Glenn had "taken me to the woodshed" over the incident.

What was most disconcerting, however, was that John wouldn't let the matter go.

For at least a couple of weeks thereafter, he rarely missed a chance to make a snide comment or snarky reference to what he obviously regarded as a major misstep, egged on, I believed, by Tipps and Veno who were still smarting from losing the media consultant argument.

Finally, I'd had enough.

I had been a good soldier and had been willing to publicly humiliate myself, but I had now eaten all the crow I could stomach.

It was time to move on, one way or another.

Early one morning I went to the senator's office and closed the door.

I apologized again for upsetting him, but said my penitence had gone on long enough and was now threatening to undercut my effectiveness in the campaign that lay ahead.

If John had lost confidence in me, it was best that I resign as campaign director, which I was prepared to do forthwith.

Glenn immediately softened.

He said that while he had been angry, he had never lost confidence in me—and certainly didn't want me to resign.

He needed me to run his campaign and as far as he was concerned, the matter was closed and the drama was over.

We shook hands, I left, and John never mentioned the incident again.

Good thing, too, since it wasn't long before DeWine was on the attack.

Continuously.

Relentlessly.

And with a ferocity that caught Glenn completely off guard.

Mostly, it was a three-pronged assault.

The first prong was that it was "time for a change."

Glenn had been in the Senate for nearly eighteen years and, the argument went, had lost touch with regular Ohioans and what they wanted.

This was one of the reasons why DeWine now conveniently supported congressional term limits, which he had firmly opposed in the past.

That the US Supreme Court had already ruled congressional term limits unconstitutional was immaterial. It was time to throw the bums out.

And in 1992, the call for term limits was all the rage among Republican candidates from one end of America to the other.

DeWine's second line of attack was on the lingering debt John still had from his failed 1984 presidential campaign.

While that was fair game, what wasn't fair were the DeWine campaign's repeated insinuations that Glenn could pay off the debt himself if he wanted to.

They were well aware that the Federal Elections Commission (FEC) barred presidential candidates who had accepted federal matching funds from contributing more than $50,000 of their own money.

They knew from our public campaign finance filings that John had already done that.

And they knew from reading our press releases that Glenn had, in fact, petitioned the FEC to let him pay off the remaining debt himself—but that the FEC had turned him down.

But hey, this was politics.

And in politics, you never let facts get in the way of a good argument—or an effective line of attack against your opponent.

In reality, the whole Glenn-won't-pay-his-bills schtick was wildly misleading.

Not only had almost all of the campaign's mom-and-pop vendors been paid what they were owed, but the four Ohio banks that had loaned the campaign a total of $2 million had gotten their entire principal back.

The only thing the banks were still owed was interest on the loan—which they petitioned the FEC to let them forgive so they could close their books.

But once again the FEC refused, ruling that such an arrangement would constitute an illegal campaign contribution to the Glenn for President campaign.

Nevertheless, the debt-related attacks rolled on unabated—and eventually began to take a toll, courtesy of a clever TV ad campaign that I'll get to in a moment.

The third prong in the DeWine attack was John's involvement in the Keating Five affair.

In actuality, to borrow Gertrude Stein's wry observation about Oakland, there wasn't much there, there.

After a thorough investigation by the special counsel they'd hired, the Senate Ethics Committee had essentially cleared Glenn of wrongdoing, giving him only a mild slap on the wrist for having exercised "poor judgment" in setting up a meeting between Keating and Speaker of the House Jim Wright.

But again, this was politics.

And the Keating matter nicely dovetailed with the DeWine campaign's "time for a change" theme.

All of which meant that John being cleared of wrongdoing wasn't going to stop Greg Stevens and his media team from going for John's jugular with over-the-top TV spots featuring side-by-side photos of Glenn and the now criminally charged Charles Keating, resplendent, as I recall, in an orange prison jumpsuit, with his police booking numbers below his mugshot.

The message wasn't exactly subtle.

If Glenn wasn't a criminal himself, he was at least criminally adjacent.

Or as DeWine himself often put it: "What happened to the John Glenn we used to know?"

That this kind of take-no-prisoners assault stunned John would come as no surprise to those aware of his near-Pollyannaish view of politics.

Flower Power?

Before returning to the campaign, permit me another brief detour.

Though President Kennedy often remarked that "politics ain't beanbag," his brother Bobby (who was no stranger to sharp-elbowed political tactics and was often called "ruthless" early in his career) later preferred to focus on the good things that government action could achieve, especially for those who are marginalized and live in the shadows of our society.

He often said, and by most accounts truly believed, that politics could be a "noble profession."

John Glenn wholeheartedly embraced this view, along with a corollary conviction that politicians who do good work should be rewarded by the voters, and not criticized too harshly by their opponents.

His wanting to believe everyone else felt the same way sometimes led to amusing results.

As in 1992 when we placed a bet on whether he or DeWine would get the editorial endorsement of *The Columbus Dispatch.*

The *Dispatch*, which had the second-largest circulation in the state, was then a family-owned paper (it has since been sold to Gatehouse Media, a subsidiary of Gannett) run with an iron fist for 123 years by the rock-ribbed Republican Wolfe family.

In the early '90s, the publisher was John F. Wolfe, who took the reins after the death of his cousin—John W. Wolfe—and was among the handful of "titans" who sat atop Columbus's civic and political landscape.

That the Wolfes also owned WBNS-TV (the CBS network affiliate in Columbus) and WBNS radio, one of the city's top-rated radio stations, only added to their influence.

The Wolfes may not have had a media monopoly in Ohio's capital city, but they certainly had an oligopoly—which they unfailingly used to benefit Republicans.

By 1992, it had been eighty years since their newspaper had endorsed a Democrat for president.

And *Dispatch* endorsements for Democratic US Senate candidates were only slightly easier to come by.

All of which explains why John was a bit surprised when Wolfe called him in 1991—a year before his reelection campaign—to ask for his assistance.

To commemorate the 500th anniversary of Christopher Columbus's arrival in America, Wolfe had decided the state's capital city should host an international horticultural exposition, which he dubbed "AmeriFlora."

It would be, Wolfe said, the first international flower show in the United States—and making it happen was vitally important to him.

But there was a catch.

AmeriFlora had to be sanctioned by the International Association of Horticultural Producers if it was to be officially recognized and able to attract foreign growers and sponsors.

The competition for that seal of approval would be fierce, and an in-person presentation by AmeriFlora backers would be necessary.

But the Association was located in the Netherlands—and in Amsterdam, of course, nobody had ever heard of John F. Wolfe.

But they had certainly heard of John Glenn.

Might John be willing to travel with Wolfe and his delegation to help sell AmeriFlora to the Dutch?

Glenn jumped at the opportunity. Bringing an international flower show to Columbus would be good for the city. And it would significantly boost his chances of getting a reelection endorsement from the *Dispatch*.

Or so he thought.

Wolfe's gambit worked—at least for Wolfe.

The European flower honchos were suitably impressed by John's presence—and when the pollen settled, AmeriFlora was sanctioned for a two-week international indoor competition.

That wasn't as long a period as AmeriFlora's backers wanted, but it was certainly better than nothing—and they finally had the international recognition they so desperately sought.

Surely, Glenn thought, John F. Wolfe would be grateful enough to reward him with a *Dispatch* endorsement of his reelection.

I thought otherwise and told him so.

When push comes to shove, I said, Wolfe is a Republican before he is anything else.

And come November, he would endorse the GOP candidate for Senate just as he almost always did.

John was so sure I was wrong that he demanded we put a wager on it.

If he got the *Dispatch* endorsement, he won. If DeWine was endorsed, I won.

The stakes were a dinner for four (Annie and my wife, Vicki, would join us) at a Columbus restaurant of the winner's choosing.

When the *Dispatch* endorsed DeWine that fall, you might think that my wife and I at least got a splendid meal at an upscale restaurant out of it.

You would be wrong. Vicki and I never collected on the dinner.

John was so irate over what he saw as Wolfe's partisan pettiness that I could never summon the requisite courage to ask him to pay up.

Parenthetically, I should note that AmeriFlora turned out to be something of a bust.

The show cost a far-over-budget $95 million to stage, was plagued by days of torrential rain that flooded its lagoons, and drew public protests from both African Americans (whose city park was commandeered to host the festival) and Native Americans (who were affronted by the celebration of Christopher Columbus).

It was a financial fiasco.

Karma, as they say, is a bitch.

A sad day, as John and I go over his remarks on withdrawing from the 1984 presidential campaign.

John reviews notes with his press secretary before a 1985 news conference outside the Capitol. *Photo by Ron Kuntz, used with permission of his estate*

Senator John Glenn and I, his often clueless "copilot," stand alongside his twin-engine Beechcraft Baron in 1986.

Engulfed in a sea of confetti, John and Annie were caught off guard by the surprise party I organized in the Senate for the twenty-fifth anniversary of his orbital space flight in 1987. *Photo courtesy of the US Senate*

As MC for the party, I spoke of John's heroism aboard Friendship 7. *Photo courtesy of the US Senate*

John always had a way with kids, including mine.

Howard and I discuss his victory speech on election night in 1988.

My family visits with Massachusetts Senator Ted Kennedy during a trip to Washington in 1991.

Fast food too often fuels political campaigns, as it did in this strategy meeting for Glenn's 1992 Senate reelection campaign.

Watching the returns come in on election night in 1992.

On election night in 1992, the Glenns and I celebrate John's election to a fourth term in the Senate.

Annie and my wife Vicki share a quiet moment in 1992.

With my daughter Danielle and sons Brodie and Shane, I visited with Al Gore just before his election as vice president in 1992.

Senator Metzenbaum hosts my family at his Senate office in 1993. An entire wall was reserved for photos of his staff's children, whom he called "Metzenbabies."

Vicki joined me on the floor of the 1996 Democratic National Convention in Chicago.

John talks with my family after a 1996 presidential campaign rally in Ohio.

Discussing strategy with Jene Galvin and Jerry Springer in 2003. *Photo by Michael E. Keating, used with permission from* The Cincinnati Enquirer

In 2003, Jerry Springer created a stir at Upper Arlington High School when he watched my son Shane play baseball. Before the game he visited with my son Chad and his wife, Angie.

On a 2024 class trip to Washington, my granddaughter Olivia visited John Glenn's grave at Arlington National Cemetery. *Photo courtesy of the Skestos family*

Chapter Sixteen

The 1992 Reelection Campaign, Part III

THE GLENN CAMPAIGN PARRIED OUR opponent's time-for-a-change term-limit argument by pointing out that DeWine was against term limits before he supported them—and that he was hardly in a position to decry "career politicians" when he himself had never held a single nonpolitical or nonelective job during his entire adult life.

We also went on offense by pointing out that DeWine's years in Congress weren't exactly marked by legislative distinction.

Outside of a handful of bills he authored that renamed a few post offices or declared certain calendar dates as National This-or-That Day, DeWine's legislative cupboard was embarrassingly bare.

We also hammered DeWine—in both the free and paid media—for his staunch antichoice stand on the abortion issue.

He was a fervid Right-to-Lifer whose antichoice convictions were, even in the years before *Roe* was overturned, a minority view in Ohio.

One of our most effective ads was a Glenn-to-camera spot in which the senator contrasted his views and voting record with those of DeWine, with the difference being that John believed decisions concerning whether and when to begin a family or when an abortion was medically necessary should rest with the woman and her doctors, not a bunch of politicians and bureaucrats.

It ended with Glenn looking directly into the eyes of the viewers and declaring, "I trust the women of Ohio."

When that ad began to have an impact, DeWine sought to counter it with a thirty-second spot featuring his wife, Fran, who assured Ohioans that while her husband's position on choice was controversial, it was sincerely held and should not be counted against him.

And on it went until September, when the race was suddenly turned upside down by a series of ads from Greg Stevens themed around Glenn's presidential campaign debt.

It was a brilliant concept that played off a widely known Energizer battery ad campaign that had been airing on television for several years.

The corporate ads featured a battery-powered stuffed bunny parading around in circles beating a drum, while an off-camera announcer declaimed that Energizers kept "going and going and going."

Stevens's ads used a look-alike bunny also beating a drum and walking in circles.

Except his sported a Glenn name tag as the announcer intoned, "John Glenn. He keeps owing... and owing... and owing."

It was creative, funny—and devastatingly effective.

People were talking about the ad. It was seriously cutting into our lead (more about that in a minute), and worst of all, we didn't have an answer that would fit into a thirty-second reply spot.

And then the DeWine campaign overstepped.

Obviously pleased with the havoc their "bunny" ads had created for us, Stevens and company couldn't resist visiting one last indignity on Glenn.

They aired an ad in which their Energizer Bunny was decked out in a space suit and helmet.

It was an act of pure hubris. And as the ancient Greeks reminded us, acts of hubris rarely end well.

When the *Challenger* space shuttle blew up shortly after launch in 1986, among those killed instantly was NASA astronaut—and Akron native—Judy Resnik.

Glenn knew Resnik personally and, at the request of then–Vice President George H. W. Bush, had accompanied him to Cape Canaveral on the day of the disaster to console the astronauts' family members who had watched in horror as their loved ones died on live national television.

The DeWine campaign had finally gone too far—and I sensed an opening.

I immediately issued a press release—and told every print and electronic media reporter who would listen—that putting their bunny in a space suit not only mocked the service that astronauts like Glenn had given to this country, but denigrated the memory of "heroes like Judy Resnik" who had given their lives to America's space program.

Was it a stretch? Perhaps.

But for the first time since they started airing the "bunny" ads, the DeWine campaign was on the defensive, explaining why their use of a space suit and helmet shouldn't be seen as crass, disrespectful, and inappropriate. And it is an iron law of politics that when you're forced to explain why an attack on your opponent is justified, you're losing the argument.

At the very least, the kerfuffle gave our campaign a few days of breathing room as the media weighed and sought to referee the dueling claims and counterclaims.

Meanwhile, we were pouring buckets of money into TV ads that blistered the lieutenant governor's time-for-a-change hypocrisy.

Using lurid film footage of the Las Vegas Strip as a backdrop, an announcer solemnly recounted all the campaign cash DeWine had raked in during multiple fundraising visits to Sin City.

Though trying to cast himself as a breath of fresh air, DeWine, we suggested, was in reality "just another politician."

The Energizer Bunny ads, however, kept airing.

And though I have never before disclosed this publicly, our campaign's internal polling showed that our longtime lead over DeWine had evaporated.

With nine days to go, the race was essentially tied.

The Gold Star Mother Speech Redux

Fortunately (for us) the candidates were scheduled to square off in a debate on October 26—a week before the November 3 election—which would be televised statewide.

It gave us one last opportunity to tip the scales in a race that was now tighter than a tick.

Sponsored by the League of Women Voters of Ohio, the debate was to be held at the Columbus studios of WBNS-TV, where questions would be posed by a panel of journalists.

Though WBNS was a CBS network affiliate, any TV station in Ohio was, if I'm recalling it correctly, welcome to air the rhetorical battle.

Given the stakes, our paid media adviser Bob Shrum (who had been a college debate champion himself at Georgetown University) flew to Ohio to assist me with the senator's debate prep.

They were nerve-wracking sessions.

Glenn seemed distracted and off his game, no doubt flustered by the closeness of the race, but also genuinely angry about what he regarded as DeWine's below-the-belt attacks on his honesty and character.

Uncharacteristically, he seemed unable to focus.

And despite having an excellent memory, John was clearly having difficulty retaining the facts, figures, and talking points Shrum and I were providing.

The debate was on a Monday.

When Bob left Columbus to fly home the Friday before, neither of us knew what to expect three days later.

Then lightning struck.

It was one of those unpredictable, out-of-the-blue, "October surprises" that can sometimes reset a campaign—and a candidate.

On Sunday afternoon, just twenty-four hours before the debate, I got a telephone call from one of our campaign staffers in Cleveland.

He told me that in the city's Eastern European ethnic neighborhoods, DeWine operatives were visiting church parking lots and depositing leaflets on car windshields.

"And what do those leaflets say?" I asked.

"Well, they say that if John Glenn had had his way, the Soviet Union would still exist and Eastern Europe would still be enslaved. Do you want me to fax one to you?"

"No," I said. "I want you to get in your car right now and drive to Columbus where you will personally hand me one of those leaflets."

By 6:30 that evening, I had the flyer. Its text was exactly as advertised.

I called John at home to brief him, and we arranged to meet at campaign headquarters early the next morning.

My gut told me it was highly unlikely that the circular had been approved by the DeWine high command.

Something that potentially explosive—and distributed the day before a televised debate, no less—was almost certainly a rogue operation carried out by overzealous Cleveland campaign operatives.

But the genesis of the leaflet didn't matter.

It was done in DeWine's name.

It had his campaign's fingerprints on it.

And it was a gift.

John and I talked for fifteen minutes or so about how and when he should bring it up in the debate.

There was less discussion about *what* John would say.

We both knew it would be an updated reprise of his "Gold Star Mothers" speech that had demolished the Senate candidacy of Howard Metzenbaum almost twenty years earlier.

On Monday morning, John carefully folded the leaflet and put it in the inside pocket of his suit jacket.

He had fire in his eyes, a bounce in his step, and a renewed sense of confidence that Shrum and I hadn't seen in two days of debate prep.

He was ready.

Both candidates and their top campaign aides arrived at the WBNS studio about an hour and a half before the debate was scheduled to begin.

The station's news director guided us on a "walk-through" of the set, took the candidates to separate holding rooms, and then led Steiner, me, and our respective assistants to the second floor, where both sides would monitor the debate from adjoining administrative offices, each of which had couches, tables, chairs, snacks, and a pair of television sets.

The two offices shared a common wall which, I would soon discover, was far from soundproof.

The debate was only minutes old when one of the moderators posed a question about the negative tone of the campaign.

John pounced.

Pulling the leaflet from his jacket, he noted that DeWine operatives had been distributing it "just yesterday in Cleveland"—and then began to read the damning accusations.

Suddenly—through the paper-thin wall that separated us—I heard the unmistakable voice of Curt Steiner virtually shrieking at his staff:

"What's that? What's Glenn got in his hand? Someone... please... tell... me... WHAT... THE... F**K... IS... THAT???"

Too late.

Glenn finished reading, then looked at DeWine.

"We both had a chance to fight communism, didn't we, Mike? I in Korea and you in Vietnam. But you never fought in Vietnam; you had a series of draft deferments instead.

"Now I've never made that an issue in this campaign, because I'm sure you had your reasons.

"But I DID go to Korea; my plane was hit by antiaircraft fire on multiple occasions; and that war put more of my friends in cemeteries than I care to count.

"So I frankly resent it when you imply that I'm somehow soft on communism, was sympathetic to the Soviet Union, or wanted to see the countries of Eastern Europe enslaved.

"So let me tell you something, Mike.

"I'm a veteran of two wars.

"And the last thing I need is lessons in patriotism from people like you."

I honestly don't remember what DeWine said in response—or what was said by either candidate on all the other issues the two combatants were asked about that night.

I doubt many people who watched that debate do, either.

Because if there's one thing I've learned after watching dozens of political debates, it's that voters don't decide who they think "won" or "lost" through a careful analysis of the arguments or via any of the formal "scoring rules" that determine the outcome of academic debates.

Political debates are often won or lost when one of the candidates makes a huge mistake—or has a "mic drop" moment.

And my candidate had just had the latter.

In that instant, the debate was over. Glenn won.

Still, there was a week to go—and John was nervous.

About four days out, he and Annie came to the campaign office around 10:00 p.m., knowing I'd still be working.

When he sat down, Glenn asked me for a cigarette.

It was the only time I ever saw him smoke.

He and Annie had been talking—and wanted to know if there was any way we could buy more TV time and air more ads.

If there wasn't enough campaign cash on hand, he'd pay for the ads himself.

And he also wondered whether we should maybe run another "bio" spot in our ad rotation, reminding voters of his lifelong service to the country.

I pointed out that we had bought all the prime TV time that was available; the only times left were in the wee hours of the morning when virtually no one was watching. Paying to air ads then would simply be a waste of money.

I also told him, as gently as I could, that if I thought another bio spot would be effective, I'd tell our media team to air one immediately.

The problem, I said, isn't that Ohioans don't know who you are.

The problem is that voters are angry at politicians this year—which is why the Republicans' "term limits" proposal is resonating all over the country.

"And what that tells me is that we can't make this race a referendum on you. We need to make it a choice between you and Mike DeWine—and the best way to do that is to keep telling voters not who *you* are, but who *he* is."

I reassured the Glenns, however, that we'd stopped the bleeding and that John's debate performance had gotten us back on track. "I think we should trust the voters. You've never let them down—and I simply don't believe they're going to let you down."

In truth, I wasn't so sure.

Though I was confident that John had, in fact, won the debate, history shows that debates usually don't move the needle very much—or for very long.

Even if one candidate gets a "bump" in the polls after a debate, it's typically ephemeral, dissipates within a few days, and the race soon returns to the *status quo ante*.

Perhaps this time would be different because the debate occurred only a week before the election. But I doubted that enough people had watched it to truly make a difference.

Moreover, the daily tracking polls Mellman had been doing were still showing an extremely close race with considerably more undecided voters than I was comfortable with.

Though those daily tracks ended the weekend before the election, conventional wisdom holds that "late deciders" almost always break for the challenger—and for a very simple reason: If the incumbent hasn't won those folks over by that point, they are likely to go in the opposite direction.

In 1992, however, the unlikely happened.

The "undecideds" ended up breaking for us—big time.

When the ballots were counted, Mike DeWine received just 42 percent of the vote.

Martha Grevatt of the far-left Workers World Party got nearly 7 percent, which almost certainly reflected the disgust many voters felt over the nasty tenor of the campaign.

It strains credulity, however, to believe Grevatt's presence on the ballot took votes away from DeWine.

Inasmuch as she was a self-described Communist, it's hard to believe that her supporters would otherwise have voted Republican.

Glenn had an incredible night, garnering 51 percent of the vote and handily beating DeWine by 9 percentage points—just 1 point shy of the 10 percent (or more) margin that is generally considered to be a "landslide."

Washington pundits and others outside our campaign operation who looked at the final vote tally doubtless concluded that it really wasn't such a tough race after all—and that Glenn had it in the bag all along.

If they only knew.

Chapter Seventeen

The 1992 Reelection Campaign, Part IV

THE IMPORTANCE OF GLENN'S WINNING margin, however, went far beyond bragging rights or his own sense of vindication.

It's also likely that Bill Clinton rode to victory in Ohio on John's coattails.

Typically, of course, it's the other way around: Down-ballot candidates are helped (or hurt) by their party's presidential candidate at the top of the ticket.

But in this case the reverse was true: Clinton won Ohio by less than two points; Glenn's nine-point win may have been just enough to drag Bill across the finish line.

What I know for sure is that Clinton would have *lost* Ohio had it not been for Glenn's intervention.

In October, Mark Mellman—who also did polling for the Clinton campaign—told John and me that because of his sagging poll numbers in the state, Clinton was on the verge of pulling his TV ads in Ohio and reallocating those dollars to other states where his campaign thought their chances of winning were better.

Understand: Pulling your advertising and "going dark" on television in the closing weeks of a campaign effectively means conceding that state to your opponent.

As it happened, John was scheduled to campaign with Clinton a few days later at a rally in Springfield, Ohio.

Following the rally—at which Glenn introduced the former Arkansas governor to a large and boisterous crowd—John asked to ride with Clinton in the motorcade taking him back to his campaign plane.

And Glenn took someone else along for that ride as well: John Block, the mercurial publisher of the family-owned *Toledo Blade* newspaper.

Block, who was also an amateur pilot, had called me several days before the Springfield event to say he would be attending and asked if I could get him a few minutes alone with Glenn.

We did him one better.

John persuaded Clinton to let Block ride with them to the airport, where the publisher got fifteen minutes of personal face time with the Democratic candidate for president of the United States.

And that paid a huge if unexpected dividend, which I'll explain in a moment.

Once Block exited the plane, John sat alone with Clinton. Though I wasn't there to hear the conversation, Glenn told me later that he spoke to the Democratic presidential nominee "like a Dutch uncle."

"I told him we'd heard through the grapevine that he was thinking about pulling out of Ohio," Glenn related. "And I told him that would be a huge mistake. I felt sure he could win here—and I urged him as strongly as I could to keep his television ads on the air."

Clinton took the advice—and ended up winning Ohio and its twenty-one electoral votes by the slimmest of margins, all but ensuring his election as president.

Clinton didn't hesitate to credit Glenn for his victory in the Buckeye State.

Indeed, shortly after he was sworn in, the new president sent John a framed picture of the two of them together at that rally in Springfield.

On it, he inscribed: "To John, who never let me give up on Ohio."

For his part, John Block had been utterly charmed by Clinton in the few minutes they spent talking.

What followed was not just an editorial endorsement, but a positively glowing one that ran on the *front page* of Block's newspaper.

A few days before the election, I was campaigning with Glenn in Youngstown when my office told me that Block had called, said it was urgent, and asked that I return his call right away.

When I got him on the phone, Block said that he'd been looking at the polls and the race in Ohio seemed very tight and could go either way.

Did I think it would help if he ran his endorsement of Clinton on the front page of *The Blade* again?

"Well, it certainly wouldn't hurt, Mr. Block," I answered. "So yes, I think you should."

He did.

On election day, both Glenn and Clinton carried Lucas County by hefty margins.

A Politician's Politician

In February 1993—just three months after he was elected—Clinton returned to Ohio to hold a town hall meeting in Chillicothe, a medium-sized town that had served as the state's first capital and is located about an hour south of Columbus.

Having met and watched Clinton in action several times on the campaign trail, I was suitably impressed with his skills as a politician.

But in the gymnasium of Chillicothe High School on that cold winter day, I was utterly blown away.

Not just with Clinton's grasp of policy, but with his unparallelled ability to explain even the most complex and nuanced of issues in language readily comprehensible to everyday people.

It was a *tour de force* that I've never seen replicated by any other politician.

Clinton didn't give a speech. Instead, sitting on a stool in the middle of the gym and armed only with a handheld microphone, he took questions from the audience about anything they wished to discuss.

Questions ranged from agriculture policy to international relations to Clinton's position on abortion—and everything in between.

It went on for well over an hour, with the president randomly pointing to people sitting in the bleachers and calling on them to ask their question.

Clinton never used a note.

Facts and statistics rolled off his tongue effortlessly.

He was concise. He was to the point. He was eloquent.

And even in this more conservative corner of Ohio, he was eminently likable.

After witnessing a performance like that, I wasn't in the least surprised when, years later, grateful Democrats lauded Clinton's speeches at several national conventions by affectionately dubbing him the party's "Explainer-in-Chief." I saw an early version of that in southern Ohio.

Because it involved me, I hope you'll indulge one last vignette about Clinton's unrivaled political skills.

On the campaign trail and running for reelection in 1996, Clinton was the keynote speaker at a statewide dinner hosted by the Ohio Democratic Party.

As the state's senior Democratic officeholder, Glenn was asked to introduce him and, as always, I was tasked with writing the senator's remarks.

At the time, congressional Republicans were doing what congressional Republicans often do: pushing tax cuts that favored the wealthy and budget cuts for everyone else.

On the GOP's proposed chopping block were, among other things, cuts for preschool, school lunch, and college loan programs—and slashed federal support for the Corporation for Public Broadcasting, which aired the enormously popular *Sesame Street* television show.

In his speech, Glenn praised the president for opposing these cuts, and wondered how Republicans could pose as champions of children when they wanted to "take Big Bird away from two-year-olds, kindergarten away from five-year-olds, school lunches away from twelve-year-olds, and college loans away from eighteen-year-olds."

When the event concluded, deep-pocketed Democratic Party donors were led backstage to participate in a time-honored political ritual: the "grip and grin" photo—otherwise known even less formally as well-heeled big shots having their picture taken with the guest of honor—in this case, the president of the United States.

Not being major financial contributors, Vicki and I were standing in the back of the room waiting for Senator Glenn, who was also having his picture taken with donor heavyweights.

In time, a Clinton staffer approached us and said he was sure the president wouldn't mind if we joined the line to have our picture taken, too.

Appreciative, we went to the back and were, literally, the last people in line.

When it was finally our turn, Vicki introduced herself to the president, shook his hand, and took her position immediately to his right.

I followed suit—but I had no sooner introduced myself when Clinton said (I swear I'm not making this up):

"So you're the famous Dale Butland I've heard so much about.

"Take 'Big Bird away from two-year-olds, kindergarten away from five-year-olds, school lunches away from twelve-year-olds, and college loans away from eighteen-year-olds.'

"That's great stuff.

"Would you mind if I borrowed that line and used it myself?"

Utterly stunned that Clinton would even know my name, let alone be able to recite verbatim something I'd written, I picked my jaw off the floor and, completely tongue-tied, mumbled something along the lines of "No, Mr. President, I'd be honored if you were to do that."

Clearly, the man did his homework. Another mark of a great politician.

Chapter Eighteen

The 1994 Senate Campaign

On the Loan Again (apologies to Willie Nelson)

DESPITE SUCH MOMENTOUS EVENTS AS the inauguration of a new president, Clinton's "don't ask, don't tell" compromise on gays serving in the military, the shoot-out at the Branch Davidian compound in Texas, and the bombing of the World Trade Center in New York City (which turned out to be a dress rehearsal for the 9/11 catastrophe), 1993 was a relatively uneventful year for Glenn personally.

That November, however, I got a call from Joel Hyatt, an ultrasuccessful legal entrepreneur and Howard Metzenbaum's son-in-law, asking me to meet with them at Joel's ski home in Colorado just before Thanksgiving.

Only a handful of people were invited—and the purpose was to discuss a possible Hyatt Senate campaign in 1994 if Howard chose not to seek reelection.

I went.

"It won't be a cakewalk," I predicted. "For one thing, voters don't like nepotism or politicians trying to hand their offices off to relatives. Beyond that, Joel, you've never held an elective office of any kind—and even a lot of Democrats are going to complain that you're an interloper who hasn't paid his dues."

Hyatt said he had already thought about both of those things.

And while agreeing that they were potential problems, he believed they could be overcome with a strong campaign, the huge campaign war chest he expected to have on the day he announced his candidacy, and the fulsome support he was sure he'd get from the Clinton White House, where he and Howard had numerous connections.

Metzenbaum mostly listened and didn't say much.

To be honest, I wasn't sure Howard actually *wanted* to retire and got the sense that he hadn't yet made an irrevocable decision.

The confab ended with everyone promising to keep an open mind and to continue thinking about the matter.

In early 1994, Metzenbaum announced he would retire, Hyatt announced he would run, and that his campaign team would not include me, Peter Harris, or anyone else who had held a senior position in Howard's 1988 reelection effort.

Evidently, Joel had concluded the best way to blunt the nepotism issue was by populating his campaign staff with new faces unassociated with his father-in-law.

It didn't work.

Joel's announcement was immediately met with a chorus of complaints by Democratic officeholders who *had* "paid their dues," insisted that Ohio doesn't "pass down US Senate seats," lampooned his lack of experience, and wondered aloud "Who does Hyatt think he is?"

Contrary to Joel's expectations, the fact that he had, indeed, already raised several million dollars in campaign cash did not scare everyone off.

Shortly after Hyatt's announcement, a Cuyahoga County commissioner from Cleveland named Mary Boyle threw her bonnet into the ring, announcing that she would challenge Joel in the primary and that her campaign would be managed by Jerry Austin.

But Joel Hyatt's problems went far beyond nepotism.

A double Ivy League graduate (Dartmouth, Yale Law School), Hyatt—who came from humble socioeconomic roots—had become a self-made millionaire by founding Hyatt Legal Services, a national chain of storefront law offices that kept client-friendly business hours and provided simple legal services (like wills and uncomplicated divorces) at set prices, thus making them affordable and accessible to millions of middle- and low-income clients who had hitherto been priced out of the market.

But his real genius lay in pioneering something the hidebound legal profession at that time Simply Did Not Do.

He *advertised.*

More specifically, he spent millions of dollars airing dozens upon dozens of television ads featuring himself, which unfailingly ended with his iconic slogan: "I'm Joel Hyatt—and you have my word on it."

Because his ubiquitous TV ads had been running for years prior to his Senate bid, Joel reasonably believed that the worker-friendly nature of his business—coupled with the high name recognition he had built—would greatly aid his bid for public office.

As it turned out, the ads were a double-edged sword.

Though voters knew his name, they also knew Joel as not only a *lawyer*, but a smooth-talking *celebrity* lawyer at that.

Add in that he was now also a *politician*, and Joel had, for many voters, won the mistrust trifecta.

Then there was Hyatt's sometimes abrasive personality.

Personally, I always got along well with Joel—and we remain good friends to this day.

He's smart, articulate, policy savvy, and an exceptionally quick study.

But Joel doesn't suffer fools gladly and virtually reeks with self-confidence, neither of which sits particularly well with a lot of people.

Though largely unknown and little more than a cipher among voters statewide, Mary Boyle—under the tutelage of Austin—ran a low-budget but surprisingly effective campaign squarely centered on Hyatt's vulnerabilities.

Like Washington State's Patty Murray, who two years earlier had parlayed her "just a mom in tennis shoes" slogan into winning a US Senate seat, Boyle ran on a knockoff "mom versus millionaire" theme.

She nearly made it work.

When the votes were counted, Hyatt, who had outspent Boyle from hell to breakfast, squeaked past her by less than two percentage points, 46.25 to 44.48 percent.

On the Republican side, Mike DeWine, Glenn's 1992 nemesis, beat back a well-funded challenge by Cleveland cardiologist Bernadine Healy to once again become the GOP's Senate nominee.

Shaken by barely surviving the primary, Hyatt swiftly opted to get the Metzenbaum campaign band back together again.

He fired his primary election staff and hired Peter Harris as his campaign manager, Mark Mellman as his pollster, and Doak & Shrum as his paid media firm.

He also asked Peter to find out if I'd be willing to sign on as campaign communications director.

I knew the 1994 election was shaping up as a tough year for Democrats and that we would be hard pressed to keep our Senate majority.

President Clinton, as is often the case for incumbents in midterm elections, was unpopular, and there were a record number of open seats with no sitting Democratic senator in the running.

I told Peter I would take the job—but only, of course, if Glenn were willing to again put me "on loan."

After calls from both Metzenbaum and Hyatt, John consented.

In late May—with just over five months to go before the general election—the team that had guided Metzenbaum to victory six years earlier went to work for his son-in-law.

Hyatt had plenty of money—and was a far better campaigner than Mike DeWine.

The latter point was conceded even by longtime Ohio GOP Party Chairman Bob Bennett (no relation to the same-named special prosecutor for the Senate Ethics Committee), who remarked: "Our guy is pretty dull. But that's Ohio. We don't like glitz much and we don't take fliers. We like to be near the top, but never out front."

Joel was a good candidate and we ran a good race.

Though Hyatt (perhaps unwisely) was adamant about keeping Metzenbaum on the sidelines to mitigate the nepotism issue, Glenn did everything he could to help, even flying Joel and me in his Beech Baron to six different cities in two days—and introducing him at each stop as we kicked off Joel's general election campaign.

But after four decades in politics, I've learned that sometimes even the best campaigns and candidates get caught in tides of history they can't escape.

It has often been said that in life, timing is the most crucial element of success.

But in politics—as in stand-up comedy—timing is *everything.*

Running for election in the right year means bad candidates often win.

Running in the wrong year means good candidates often lose.

And 1994 was a flat-out terrible year for Democrats.

Polls showed we trailed DeWine for the entire campaign. And when the smoke cleared on election night, we were swamped by 14 points, losing 53 percent to 39 percent.

There was at least some small solace in knowing it wasn't just us—it was a disaster for Democrats across the board from sea to shining sea.

No sitting Republican senator lost, while the GOP managed to defeat two Democratic incumbents.

And Republicans also won *every single one* of those six open Senate seats.

Democrats started the year with a 56–44 Senate majority. We ended it in the minority, holding just 46 seats.

It was, to use a technical term, an old-fashioned butt-kicking.

Chapter Nineteen

Jerry Springer and the Senate Campaign That Wasn't

BEFORE RETURNING TO MY REMAINING years with John Glenn, I hope you'll permit me another detour, even if it is chronologically out of order.

Though I've worked for many politicians and political causes over the past forty-five years, the primary focus of this book has been my experiences with two former US senators—John Glenn and Howard Metzenbaum.

However, another person for whom I worked—but who ultimately chose *not* to run for the Senate—was, in many ways and for many reasons, equally fascinating.

His name was Jerry Springer.

Yes, *that* Jerry Springer.

Some of what follows I've never mentioned publicly before; other observations were incorporated into an op-ed I wrote for *The Cincinnati Enquirer* shortly after Jerry died from cancer in April 2023.

Most Ohioans, like most Americans, only knew Jerry Springer as the host of a much-ridiculed eponymous television show that was the epitome of what frequently was called "Trash TV."

Routinely featuring freakish guests who often occupied the most downscale rungs on America's socioeconomic ladder (and talked about such outrageously taboo topics as "I Married a Horse"), the nationally syndicated *Jerry Springer Show* was sometimes raunchy, frequently ribald, and always raucous.

And that show is precisely why Jerry was so easily dismissed by Very Serious People.

But there was another and far more complex side to Springer—a lawyer, former mayor of Cincinnati, and Emmy-winning newscaster at WLWT-TV in that city—who once seriously considered running for the US Senate in Ohio.

The serious Jerry Springer was the one who hired me to serve as communications director for his 2004 Senate exploratory campaign.

And it is *that* Jerry Springer who I believe merits a few pages in this book.

I first met Jerry in early 2003 after several news outlets reported that he was contemplating a Senate bid—and shortly after I wrote an opinion column for *The Columbus Dispatch* suggesting that those who openly scoffed at his chances might be a bit premature.

How seriously he should be taken, I wrote, depends on "whether Springer throws his hat or his chair into the ring."

A few days after that op-ed was published, I got a call from Tim Burke—a longtime Springer ally and chairman of the Hamilton County Democratic Party—who told me Jerry had seen the column and wanted to know if I would meet with him.

About a week later, Jerry and I had a two-hour breakfast at a downtown Cincinnati hotel.

I was thoroughly impressed with what I heard.

Like me, John Glenn, and so many others, he had been inspired by Bobby Kennedy and worked in his 1968 presidential campaign. After the assassination, Jerry moved to Cincinnati, where he was elected to the city council in 1971—and then as mayor several years later.

After an unsuccessful run for Ohio governor in 1982, Springer quit politics to become a Cincinnati TV news anchor—and nine years later relocated to Chicago to host his improbably successful daytime television show.

But he had never lost his interest in government—and thought maybe now he could use his celebrity to win a Senate seat where he could be a voice and a vote for the causes that truly count.

Not only was Springer passionate and knowledgeable about major domestic and international issues, he was also articulate, thoughtful, and humble enough to realize he didn't have all the answers.

And that's where he hoped I would come in.

Pulling this off, he said, would require that he have the advice and counsel of someone who knew Ohio politics and had experience in running a successful US Senate campaign in the state.

What I found particularly striking was that Springer was self-aware enough to fear that what he called his "silly show" might well disqualify him as a candidate in the minds of many voters.

His plan was to launch an exploratory campaign that would be run by the late Mike Ford, his longtime friend and political *consigliere* when Springer served as Cincinnati mayor and a city councilman in the 1970s and '80s. Ford had gone on to have a successful political consulting career and lived in the Washington, DC area.

Jerry, who was now a wealthy man several times over, was prepared to self-finance the entire effort, which would include extensive polling and focus groups, as well as nonstop travel, speeches, editorial board meetings, and personal appearances throughout Ohio.

And though he and his wife, Micki Velton, resided in Florida (Springer rented an apartment at the John Hancock building in downtown Chicago when taping his television show), Jerry was fully prepared to buy a home and move back to Cincinnati if our research showed he could be a viable candidate.

At the end of our meeting, Jerry asked that I sign on as communications director and senior adviser—and made it clear he was willing to pay me handsomely.

Now retired from the Senate, running my own consulting company, and largely out of the campaign business, I asked for a few days to think it over.

I desperately wanted to see at least one of Ohio's Senate seats back in Democratic hands and used those few days to consider what alternatives there might be.

I frankly came up empty.

The truth was that after years in the political wilderness, the Ohio Democratic Party had a pretty shallow bench.

And we had *nobody* whose name recognition was anywhere close to Springer's, let alone anyone who possessed his ability to attract media attention and generate excitement.

Maybe it was time to start thinking outside the box.

Since we weren't winning with conventional candidates, maybe it was time to try an unconventional one.

We had nothing to lose.

After all, it had been eleven years since Ohio had last elected a Democrat to the US Senate.

I called Jerry and joined the Springer for Senate Exploratory Campaign.

Oh, and there was one more thing that deeply impressed me about Jerry at that breakfast meeting.

It's All a Gift

When we left the restaurant, there was a homeless man on the street holding a cup and asking passersby for any spare change they might have.

Without interrupting his conversation with me, Jerry pulled a $100 bill from his wallet and dropped it into the cup, never waiting for thanks or slowing his stride.

True, a hundred dollars to a multimillionaire may be like ten bucks to the rest of us. Still, it was just the first of many times I would see his compassion and personal generosity toward those down on their luck and living difficult lives.

A story Jerry shared with me several weeks after I joined his exploratory effort went a long way toward explaining why.

In the 1980s—while still a newsman at WLWT-TV in Cincinnati—Springer had traveled to Ethiopia, both to report on the deadly famine that was decimating that country and to distribute donations of food, water, and medicine that his television station had helped coordinate.

"In the village we visited," he told me, "a majority of the children died before they reached their twelfth birthday. It didn't matter how smart they were or what kinds of talents they might have. If they were unlucky enough to be born in that village, they probably wouldn't reach adulthood.

"Here in the United States, of course, those of us who do well in life like to tell ourselves that we're responsible for our own success. 'We have talent,' we say. 'We're willing to work hard.'

"Well, a lot of people in this world have talent. A lot of people work hard. I work hard. But if I had been born in that Ethiopian village, how hard I was willing to work wouldn't matter. Because I would probably be dead before I reached the age of twelve.

"None of us choose our parents or where we're born. We're either lucky or we're not. At the end of the day, it's all a gift."

~

Though he was whip smart and highly educated (Tulane undergrad; Northwestern University Law School), intelligence wasn't what made Jerry such a potentially formidable candidate.

After nearly half a century in Ohio politics working for such giants as John Glenn and Howard Metzenbaum, I never met anyone with more charisma, better on-camera communication skills, or a more genuine connection with working-class voters than Jerry Springer.

Ironically, the latter was largely a by-product of his "silly show."

Though Springer's political base in Cincinnati had always been in the city's blue-collar west side, *The Jerry Springer Show* was what endeared him to low- and middle-income people all across Ohio and the nation.

While the intelligentsia saw him as the ringmaster of a depraved television circus exploiting mostly downscale people talking about shameful things not discussed in polite society, his enormous audience (at one time, *The Jerry Springer Show* aired in more than 190 US markets, was broadcast in 50 foreign countries, and was the most-watched television program on planet Earth) saw a sympathetic and nonjudgmental host who championed regular people and never mocked or looked down on them.

Jerry's appeal to these folks—and the trust they had in him—was on full display in the many focus groups we conducted around Ohio as he considered a Senate bid.

But it wasn't confined to Ohio—and you didn't need a focus group to see it.

At the 2004 National Democratic Convention in Boston (at which we had arranged for him to serve as an unpaid reporter/analyst for a Cleveland television station), Jerry agreed to speak on presidential nominee John Kerry's behalf at a *Rock the Vote* event across the street from Fenway Park—on a summer night when the New York Yankees were in town to play the Red Sox.

As baseball fans know, the Yankees/Red Sox rivalry is among the most intense in all of sports, and every game between the two teams is sold out months in advance.

But Jerry (who was a lifelong Yankees fan, having grown up in Queens, New York, after his family fled Poland to escape the Holocaust) somehow managed to secure three outrageously priced tickets so he, I, and Jene Galvin—his dearest friend and campaign "body man"—could go to the ballgame after the speech.

We arrived in the fourth inning and entered the park on the third-base side of the stadium. Our seats, however, were on the first-base side of the field, which required us to walk nearly halfway around the sold-out stadium in front of a crowd riveted on the game.

They were riveted on the game, that is, until they saw Jerry.

At which point a tidal wave of fans poured into the aisles yelling "Jer-ry, Jer-ry" as they made their way toward Springer clutching game programs or anything else they deemed suitable for him to sign. The heaving mob clogged the aisles and made it impossible for us to reach our seats until a phalanx of frantic ushers finally managed to restore order.

Get Back Behind the Plate

Despite his fame and the public adulation he often received, Jerry—unlike a lot of media celebrities—never took himself too seriously and was charmingly self-effacing.

Shortly after our Fenway Park experience, for example, Springer told me of his participation several years before in a Yankees Fantasy Camp at the team's spring training facility in Tampa, Florida, which his wife had bought for him as a birthday gift.

"It was so cool," he said. "On the last day of the camp, we got to play in a Yankee Legends exhibition game at George Steinbrenner Field. We campers were mixed in with the retired baseball 'legends'—and the game was always a sellout since so many fans wanted to see their favorite old-timers back in pinstripes again.

"On the team I was assigned to, I was the catcher and Whitey Ford was the pitcher.

"The third or fourth batter up for the opposing team was my childhood hero, Mickey Mantle.

"I got so excited being that close to The Mick that my glasses started to fog up and I literally couldn't see anything.

"I didn't know what else to do, so I called 'time out'—and walked out to the mound to talk with Whitey.

"I told him that Mantle had always been my all-time favorite player and explained that my glasses were fogging up and I was afraid I wouldn't be able to see Ford's pitches.

"Whitey stepped off the mound and put his arm around my shoulders.

"I knew all the fans up in the stands probably thought we were talking strategy.

"But what Ford actually said to me was: 'Springer, Mantle hasn't had a bat in his hand in at least three years—and he's drunk on his ass. Get the f**k back behind the plate.'"

The Exploitation Business

My favorite Springer story, though, concerns an editorial board meeting we had at *The Columbus Dispatch* in 2003.

As I indicated earlier, the *Dispatch* was arguably the most conservative paper in the state and its publisher was the ultra-Republican John F. Wolfe, whose equally GOP-centric family had owned the paper for well over a century.

When the *Dispatch* first asked to meet with Jerry, I warned him it would be rough sledding and that any editorial emerging from the meeting would likely tear him limb from limb.

Springer wasn't fazed in the least. "Set it up," he said. "I'm looking forward to it."

When the day came, Jerry and I were ushered into the *Dispatch's* ornate conference room in which at least a dozen editors, political reporters, and the publisher himself had gathered.

To understand how unusual this was, it's necessary to know that most editorial board meetings consist of the person being interviewed, the paper's editorial page editor and—at most—two or three other editors and/or reporters.

For this meeting, however, the room and its conference table were jammed to capacity.

And they were obviously loaded for bear.

As Jerry and I took our seats—he at one end of the conference table, and me in a chair behind him near a window—the room was so deathly quiet that the only audible sound came from the pendulum of the antique grandfather clock mounted on one of the walls.

Seated at the other end of the table to Wolfe's right, the managing editor began what can only be described as the Spanish Inquisition disguised as an interview.

"Thank you for coming, Mr. Springer," he began. "Let's get started."

Having attended dozens of editorial board meetings over the years, I knew they customarily begin by asking the guest if he or she would like to make some opening remarks—and, if they're candidates for political office, to explain why they're running and what they hope to accomplish if elected. Questions then follow.

Not this time.

The editor wasted no time moving in for the kill.

"Mr. Springer, we all know that you love to pose as a champion of the little guy—a friend of the down-and-out. Yet those are the very people whom you exploit every day on your television show—and you do it for money. How do you reconcile this contradiction?"

I shrank in my seat. This was going to be even worse than I thought.

"Well, I have a confession to make," Jerry began, smiling at his inquisitors.

"I used to be in the exploitation business. But then I gave up doing the news."

I had to stifle a laugh as Wolfe & Company looked stunned and suddenly sat up straight. This wasn't at all what they expected.

"Let me explain what I mean by that," Jerry continued.

"As many of you may know, I was a television anchor for many years at the NBC affiliate in Cincinnati. For a good part of that time, I was also the managing editor of the newsroom.

"And if our reporters caught some local official having an extramarital affair or with his hand in the cookie jar, do you think we ever hesitated in putting that on the air—or spent our morning meetings worrying about how our story might impact his family? Did we say, 'Geez, I feel badly for this guy's wife... or 'Boy, this is really going to be tough for his kids at school?'

"Hell no, we didn't do that. We couldn't wait to break the story... and were proud to have it first.

"But on *The Jerry Springer Show,* we don't do that. Nothing gets aired on my show that the guests don't personally approve and sign off on.

"In fact, if someone comes to us *after* we tape the show and says, 'You know that thing I said about my mother? I really don't think I want to see that on TV'—do you know what we do? We edit it out. Every time. No questions asked.

"Do you do that at this newspaper?

"If you interview a public official and they want to retract or modify something they said, do you accommodate them?

"I'm guessing you don't."

The *Dispatchers* stared at him blankly. No one said a word.

"And let me ask you something else," Jerry continued, "as long as we're on the topic of exploitation.

"A few years before she died, Princess Diana did a TV interview that was broadcast worldwide and was watched by millions of people. I'll bet a lot of you tuned in yourselves.

"In that interview, Diana talked about her bulimia, an extramarital affair she'd had, and the many times she'd struggled with suicidal thoughts.

"I don't recall any editorials from this or any other newspaper excoriating Princess Diana for airing her dirty laundry in public—or saying 'how dare she discuss such things on the public airwaves.'

"If you did, please tell me; I'll owe you an apology.

"But my guess is that you didn't. My guess is that you ate it up—just like all those millions of other viewers around the world.

"But see, here's the thing.

"The people who come on my show talk about those same kinds of topics.

"But of course, the people who come on my show don't dress as nicely as Diana.

"They don't speak the Queen's English.

"They aren't beautiful people.

"I guess that's what makes it different. That's what makes my show a scandal.

"I hope that answers your question. I assume you have others."

I frankly don't remember what the next question was—or any of the others that followed. But I do know they were more traditional and policy-oriented, as befitted someone contemplating a run for the US Senate.

And I also know that in all my years in politics, I never saw a candidate turn the tables on pompous and hostile interlocutors any more effectively than Jerry did—and never witnessed a media takedown even remotely close to the one I saw in Columbus that day.

In the end, Jerry decided against a Senate campaign. But I often wonder what would have happened had he run.

The political environment, of course, was different then; party discipline was still more or less intact, conventional wisdom and candidates still held sway, and the kind of rule-breaking, norm-smashing, anything-goes politics we've seen since 2016 was still a decade away.

But long before there was Donald Trump, there was Jerry Springer.

And though they appealed to the same demographic, there was also a fundamental difference.

Trump stokes grievance, hate, fear, and division.

Springer stressed empathy, understanding, and, in the words of his famous on-air sign-off, appropriated years later by NBC Nightly News anchor Lester Holt, the need to "take care of yourself and each other."

In many ways, Jerry Springer was an earlier and smarter version of Donald Trump—but without the rage, racism, and bigotry.

Had he run, I'm not sure Jerry would have been elected.

But it would have been a hell of a show.

Chapter Twenty

1995 and the Flag-Burning Amendment Fight

NOW BACK TO JOHN GLENN and the year 1995.

Since the 1960s when a few antiwar activists burned American flags to protest our nation's involvement in Vietnam, conservatives of both parties have yearned to make such protests illegal.

Indeed, many states enacted such laws in the 1970s and '80s.

In 1989, however, the US Supreme Court ruled (with archconservative Justice Antonin Scalia voting with the majority) that burning a flag in protest is a constitutionally protected right, which simultaneously rescinded all state laws that prohibited it.

That, in turn, meant that the only way to outlaw the practice was to amend the US Constitution.

But amending the Constitution isn't easily done; it requires a two-thirds majority vote in both houses of Congress and approval by three-quarters of the states.

In the years after that 1989 Supreme Court ruling, there were periodic efforts in Congress to pass an anti-flag-burning amendment, none of which succeeded.

Another such effort was mounted in the fall of 1995—and proved to be one of the most contentious and closely decided.

The proposed "Flag Desecration Amendment" read, in its entirety, "Congress shall have the power to prohibit the physical desecration of the flag of the United States."

After it passed in the House, I felt strongly that John should oppose it in the Senate.

But because he didn't share my passion on the issue—and had an almost visceral reaction to flag burners—that normally would have been the end of the story.

He was the senator and I was staff.

Nobody elected me, and what I or other staffers thought about this or any other issue was of little consequence.

In fact, my job was to defend *Glenn's* thoughts, not get him to channel mine.

I accepted that.

But I also believed that part of my job was to offer John my best judgment and policy advice—which he was then totally free to accept or reject.

It's always a delicate dance and I tried my best never to overstep.

When we disagreed, all I ever asked was a chance to make my case.

If I could bring the boss around to what I believed was the correct position or course of action, great.

If not, I had two choices.

One was to make my peace with what the senator decided and defend it vigorously and to the best of my ability with the news media or anyone else who asked.

If my conscience would not allow me to do that, my other option was to quit and find another job.

Fortunately, in the nearly twenty years I worked for him, John and I had few major disagreements, and none that reached the crisis-of-conscience threshold.

Just as important, even when we *did* disagree, John was willing to hear me out. I didn't always win the argument, of course, but I always had a chance to get my oar in.

I've often said that John Glenn was perhaps the most open-minded politician I ever worked with, which was yet another reason I so loved and respected him.

It wasn't that John was wishy-washy or easily swayed. He had strong principles, firmly held core convictions, and an unwavering sense of right and wrong.

But he also had something else that was rare in politics then—and even scarcer today.

John had a genuine sense of humility; he accepted that he might not always be right and believed he might actually benefit from hearing other points of view.

I've often reflected on where this attribute might have come from; it's certainly not something one would necessarily expect from a war hero, test pilot, and twenty-three-year Marine Corps veteran.

I've concluded that Glenn's open-mindedness may have been a byproduct of another one of his attributes; namely, his unquenchable *curiosity*, a trait he said he'd had since childhood and one he often observed in other successful people he had met and admired throughout his life.

Whether it was Robert Kennedy, the renowned heart surgeon Michael DeBakey, or rocket scientist Wernher von Braun, Glenn said the one thing they all had in common was a deep and abiding curiosity. Not just about their own chosen fields. But about *everything*.

When the original seven Mercury astronauts were invited to a dinner at von Braun's home, for example, they were first ushered into his library, where John expected to see all manner of books on physics and rocketry. Instead, the shelves were full of literature, poetry, and tomes on philosophy and religion.

Bob Kennedy, Glenn said, rarely talked about himself or his own interests. He instead was an avid listener who asked question after question of those he met, especially if their careers were outside of politics and government.

It was, therefore, hardly a surprise when John asked why I was so adamantly opposed to the flag-burning amendment.

Our discussion was a long one that spanned not just several minutes, but several hours.

I believe it would be instructive to recount much of that conversation here—not for the purpose of blowing my own horn or overstating my role in John's change of position, but because the process itself was emblematic of how Glenn approached controversial legislative matters and made momentous decisions.

More than any other incident I can recall in the two decades I worked for him, I believe John's journey on the flag-burning amendment—from supporter to opponent—best illustrates his willingness to entertain countervailing points of view, change his mind when persuaded, and fearlessly confront the political risks and consequences of standing up for what he believed was right.

Our conversation began when John asked, perhaps simply out of curiosity, why I felt so passionately about the issue.

I told him it wasn't because I sympathized with flag burners.

I didn't and I don't.

Though never comfortable with wearing my patriotism on my sleeve, I love this country deeply and cherish the ideals upon which we were founded.

Despite the many times we've fallen short or failed to live up to our principles; despite all our flaws, faults, and imperfections, I still believe the United States remains, in the immortal words of Abraham Lincoln, the world's "last, best, hope."

I have little patience with so-called progressives who never saw a foreign adversary they didn't have sympathy for—and I've never had much use for the preposterous assertion that there is some kind of moral equivalence between the US and the communist, dictatorial, or other tyrannical regimes we've opposed, past or present.

America is sometimes wrong (as we were in Vietnam), but there is a stark difference between being wrong and being evil—especially the kind of evil that inevitably results in atrocities like Hitler's Holocaust, Stalin's gulags, Pol Pot's killing fields, or Hamas's intentional slaughter of civilians at an outdoor music concert.

And that is why—even as a college student who ardently opposed the war in Vietnam—I rejected the idea that desecrating the American flag was an appropriate way to express dissent.

As I said to John, however, not everything that's *inappropriate* should be *illegal*.

The flag packs an enormous emotional wallop because it is our nation's most revered and sacred symbol, representing the myriad freedoms and liberties so many American patriots have died to protect.

But, I suggested, those who carry the Stars and Stripes into battle are not fighting to preserve a red, white, and blue piece of cloth.

They are fighting to protect the freedoms that cloth *represents*—like free speech and the right to dissent.

In other words, while the flag is a powerful symbol of our freedoms, it is only a symbol.

What a hollow and Pyrrhic victory it would be, I argued, if we were to protect the *symbol* of our freedoms by chipping away at the *actual* freedoms our flag represents.

Other leaders in other days understood this, which is why the First Amendment—which guarantees the right of all Americans to express even deeply unpopular ideas—has never been altered or amended a single time in all of American history.

Not during crises, depressions, recessions, or panics.

Not during any of our country's foreign wars—and not even during our own Civil War.

For well over two hundred years, our First Amendment has remained unchanged.

Why, exactly, should we be contemplating changing it in 1995? Was there a sudden epidemic of flag burning in the country? If so, I surely hadn't noticed it.

John nodded, then looked away in thought.

I could sense he was beginning to see the issue in a different way.

But he still had unresolved questions.

"OK," he said, "what you're saying makes sense.

"But is burning the flag really a free speech issue? Isn't there a difference between speech and action? How can burning a flag—which is an action—properly be called 'speech'?"

I said it all came down to motivation and context.

If a flag is old, soiled, or tattered, the proper way to dispose of it is by burning it.

But nobody is suggesting we make *that* illegal.

What amendment supporters were seeking to outlaw wasn't flag burning *per se*, but burning a flag in protest.

And the reason they find *that* objectionable, I proffered, is precisely because they know anyone burning a flag in protest is clearly *saying* something—in the same way that people who picket, march in protest, or use other forms of symbolic speech are saying something.

"Let's be honest," I said. "If those pushing this amendment didn't view flag burners as saying something—something they find repugnant—they wouldn't be trying to curtail the protesters' right to do it."

John didn't say anything for what seemed like several minutes.

Finally, he asked if there was anything else I'd like to add.

"Yes," I said. "I think you should also consider the *practical* implications of the proposed amendment. For one thing, it refers to 'the flag of the United States.'"

But, I pointed out, America has no "official" flag as such... and no law, regulation, or even custom spells out an exact size for the flag, or the type of material it must consist of.

Would this amendment, I wondered, apply only to defiling *manufactured* flags of a certain size—and those that are made of cloth or nylon?

What about those small, paper flags on a stick that we hand out at parades or shove into cupcakes at parties and political banquets?

Would it now be unconstitutional to toss those flags into incinerators once the events are over?

And if we're only going to prosecute people who burn flags in protest, what about a guy who says, "This flag is my personal property—and I'm going to burn it for two reasons. The first is that it's old, torn, and needs to be replaced; the second is that I want to protest that tax law Congress just passed."

Would that person be guilty of a crime?

I said I was pretty sure there were a host of other practical problems with this amendment that I hadn't yet thought of. But even the ones I identified made it clear that enforcement would become such a legal nightmare that we might as well call it The American Lawyers' Full Employment Act.

John got up from his chair, signaling that our meeting was over.

And as he often did when confronted with a difficult decision, he said he wanted to think things over.

The next day, the senator called me into his office and said he'd decided to oppose the amendment—and asked that I write a draft floor statement.

I was never prouder to be working for him than I was at that moment.

When Glenn informed Senate Minority Leader Tom Daschle of his decision, Daschle wasted no time in putting him front and center in the floor debate.

The South Dakota senator knew that amendment supporters were certain to play the patriotism card.

And he was equally certain that nobody—*nobody*—in the Senate or anywhere else could successfully out-patriot John Glenn.

Though John added many of his own thoughts to the remarks he actually delivered to his colleagues, much of what he and I discussed found its way into his floor statement.

When the Senate vote was taken on December 13, the proposed amendment—which needed a two-thirds majority to pass—was defeated by a vote of 63–36, just four votes shy of the number needed.

I am supremely confident that John's opposition—and the reasons he gave to justify it—proved persuasive to at least three of his fellow senators. And I have no doubt whatsoever that the vote would have gone the other way had John not decided to stand up and speak out.

The blowback Glenn always knew was coming was harsh and sometimes ugly.

Veterans' organizations, editorial writers, conservative radio and TV commentators, and even many of his own Ohio constituents made no secret of their displeasure with John's vote and their disappointment that he had led the charge against the amendment. Many said they held him personally responsible for its defeat.

But while he was always willing to explain his position, John never wavered, apologized, or backed away from it.

And when asked how he could possibly defend opposing a constitutional amendment that most of the people he represented supported, Glenn would simply quote from his Senate remarks:

"We don't need a First Amendment to protect *popular* speech that the majority *agrees* with. We need a First Amendment to protect *unpopular* speech that the majority *disagrees* with."

Still, I know the backlash he received deeply bothered John.

But I also know how proud he was three years later when the City Club of Cleveland—founded in 1912 as "A Citadel of Free Speech" and one of Ohio's most respected civic organizations—publicly lauded his courage and presented him with its prestigious "Guardian of Free Speech" award.

Chapter Twenty-One
Glenn Returns to Space

ON FEBRUARY 20, 1997—THE THIRTY-FIFTH anniversary of his becoming the first American to orbit the earth—John Glenn traveled to his alma mater, Muskingum College in New Concord, Ohio, to announce that he would not seek a fifth term in the United States Senate.

While he still loved the job, he would turn seventy-six in April—and, as John put it, "there is no cure for the common birthday."

For those of us who had been with him for years, it was a bittersweet moment.

On the one hand, we knew he had already given this nation a lifetime of service.

On the other hand, it was hard to believe that our own journey with this national hero would be coming to an end.

When he closed his remarks that winter afternoon, the music I chose to walk John off the stage was a song called "These Are Days" by Natalie Merchant and (the unfortunately named) 10,000 Maniacs. The lyrics perfectly captured what most of us felt; not only were the years we'd spent working with him days we would all remember, but we counted ourselves blessed and lucky to have had the privilege.

With Annie and their two adult children—Lyn and Dave—surrounding him when he finished, tears came easily, not just for his family, but for those of us who had been fortunate enough to share this incredible ride.

John's announcement marked not only the end of an era, but an end to one of the most remarkable political careers in Ohio history.

But John knew something that day the rest of us didn't.

He might not be running for reelection, but he had no intention of quietly riding off into the sunset. He still had two years left in the Senate.

With apologies to T. S. Eliot, he planned to go out not with a whimper, but with a bang.

John Glenn would be returning to space.

In retrospect, we staffers probably should have recognized that the date he picked to announce his retirement from the Senate was a clue hiding in plain sight—especially since we all knew that returning to space was something John had coveted ever since his 1962 orbital mission.

The original seven Mercury astronauts had all been promised at least two flights—and John had only gotten one.

Yet he was passed over time and again for a return to space—and no one at NASA was able (or, perhaps, willing) to tell him why.

It eventually became frustrating enough that John left the space program and retired from the Marine Corps.

Only years later did he learn why he'd been grounded.

Following his orbital triumph, Glenn was not only an international hero and one of the most celebrated figures in the world, he was also the face of an American space program that was still locked in a Cold War race to the moon with the Soviet Union.

If Glenn were to fly again and be killed, President Kennedy feared it would be a political and public relations disaster for the United States.

So, unbeknown to John, JFK quietly ordered NASA to keep him out of harm's way.

Presidential directive or not, John felt cheated.

He'd been promised a second flight—and by God, he was going to do everything in his power to redeem his dream.

For at least two years prior to announcing he would not run for reelection, John had been quietly lobbying NASA to send him back into space.

The Space Shuttle program was engaged in scientific research, and one of the things they were researching in the 1990s was the effect of space travel on the human aging process.

Glenn, who had long served as chairman of the Senate's Special Committee on Aging, saw an opportunity.

Flying an elderly person on a Space Shuttle mission made perfect sense, he argued, because some of the bodily effects of spaceflight mimic the effects of aging here on earth—such as bone density loss and a compromised immune system. Surely NASA could benefit from investigating in-flight data gleaned from someone his age.

"Besides, they already have a baseline on me," he once told me. "I'd be a perfect fit for that kind of research."

When NASA at last agreed and announced in early 1998 that John would be a payload specialist later that fall aboard the Space Shuttle *Discovery*, not everyone was enamored with the decision.

While many inside and outside the space program seemed genuinely pleased and intrigued by the prospect of Glenn becoming the oldest person ever in space, detractors dismissed it as little more than a stunt, a joyride, and an ego trip.

As John Pike, director of space policy for the Federation of American Scientists, grumpily put it: "I wish they would not confuse the issue with all this foolishness about medical research. John Glenn's first flight didn't have anything to do with science and this one doesn't either. Flying in space is about the right stuff."

As was typical of him, John ignored the critics and plowed full speed ahead.

Prior to making the announcement, of course, NASA had already done enough medical testing on Glenn to know he was fit to fly.

But he would still have to endure (and pass) the shuttle's full training protocol, which was physically taxing even for far younger astronauts.

Making it clear that he neither expected nor wanted special treatment, John threw himself into the same grueling regimen as his crewmates—and, to the surprise of no one who knew him, passed with flying colors.

On October 29, 1998, STS-95 launched from the Kennedy Space Center at Cape Canaveral with a crew of seven, one of whom was a seventy-seven-year-old space age pioneer and legend.

And as I cheekily told some Ohio reporters (once John was safely back on earth), it also marked the first time a senior citizen had left Florida in something other than a Winnebago.

Glenn's was the only space launch I ever attended, and I was fortunate to be able to witness it with my wife and children.

Though our seating in the "family section" put us far closer than the general public was allowed to be, we were still about a mile away from the launch site.

Yet even at that distance, the power of a liftoff is awe inspiring.

As the spacecraft rises from the launchpad, red-orange fire and white smoke billow from the rocket—and you can actually feel the thump of sound waves beating against your chest.

It's an unforgettable experience; all the more so if you happen to know one of the people on board.

In 1962, John spent five hours in space and orbited the earth three times.

In 1998, he was there for nine days and orbited the earth 134 times.

Happily, he got home safely both times.

But that doesn't mean there was an absence of drama when John and his STS-95 crewmates returned to earth.

For nine days, they had lived in a microgravity environment—or what the rest of us call "weightlessness." And weightlessness changes the human body.

For one thing, without the force of gravity pulling down on them, astronauts experience bone and muscle loss.

The heart adapts to the absence of gravity by shrinking in order to pump blood more efficiently. But that shrinkage also makes the heart less effective at distributing blood throughout the body when the astronauts return, often making them temporarily light-headed and dizzy.

And finally, the longer the time someone spends in space, the harder it is for their brain to readapt to the force and effect of gravity here on earth.

Added together, these three things often cause significant mobility issues for returning astronauts.

To put it starkly, many of them have difficulty walking when they exit the spacecraft.

NASA was sure that at his advanced age, Glenn would need a wheelchair—and one was waiting for him outside the shuttle.

But as Glenn later told me, "I knew the world would be watching and I was determined to walk off that craft under my own power, even if it killed me. And I'm not going to lie; it *was* hard. But I gritted my teeth and I did it."

The Right Stuff, indeed.

Chapter Twenty-Two
Glenn's Post-Senate Years

IN JANUARY 1999, JOHN'S FOURTH and final term in the Senate came to an end. But his contributions to the state and nation he loved did not.

In the fall of 1998, just a few months before he left the Senate, Ohio State University announced the creation of the John Glenn Institute for Public Service and Public Policy. Eight years later, the institute merged with the university's School of Public Policy and Management, creating the John Glenn College of Public Affairs.

Since then, the college has gained national prominence, with *U.S. News & World Report* in 2024 ranking it as the sixteenth-best public affairs school in the United States. It is the only college public affairs program in Ohio ranked among the top fifty.

Nor did John entirely leave politics behind. In retirement, he picked his spots—but wasn't shy about speaking out on behalf of issues or candidates he cared about.

In 2004, for example, he vigorously supported the presidential candidacy of John Kerry, a fellow combat veteran for whom John had first campaigned in 1984 when Kerry was elected to the Senate—and later came to deeply respect during the years they served together on Capitol Hill.

At this stage of the game, it's probably clear that I take politics very seriously.

But I don't mind admitting that I also take rock 'n' roll pretty seriously. And for me, the perfect melding of the two occurred on October 28, 2004—the day The Right Stuff met The Boss.

A little background: In the fall of that presidential election year, Bruce Springsteen and his E Street Band—along with such rock royalty as John Fogerty, James Taylor, Jackson Browne, Crosby, Stills, Nash & Young and many others—staged a series of concerts on Kerry's behalf in what they dubbed the "Vote for Change" tour.

All the concerts were held in battleground states, and the performers divided themselves into regional "teams," which allowed them to cover thirty-four cities in ten days. My wife and I attended an October 2 concert in Cleveland where we heard, among others, Springsteen, Fogerty, and R.E.M.

Though the Vote for Change tour ended in mid-October, Springsteen volunteered—given Ohio's importance in the outcome of the election—to come by himself to Columbus for one last Kerry rally, which would be held on the Ohio State University campus on October 28.

Before the event was publicly announced, Kerry called Glenn to ask if he would attend and might be interested in, oh, I don't know, introducing Bruce.

Though not entirely sure who Springsteen was, John readily agreed and shortly thereafter called to ask if I would write his intro.

As a huge Springsteen fan, I was almost giddy.

On the day of the event, everyone gathered at OSU about an hour before showtime.

Backstage, the university official in charge of coordinating the program suddenly and without warning announced that "there had been a slight change" in who would be doing what.

Specifically, the university's powers-that-be had "decided" that instead of Glenn introducing Springsteen, John would introduce an OSU student body leader who would then "have the honor" of introducing The Boss.

"No!" Springsteen emphatically interjected, almost shouting. "This is the first time I've had a chance to be introduced by a genuine national hero—and I'm not going to blow it."

Faster than you can say "Tenth Avenue Freeze-Out," the original speaking order was restored and the no doubt disappointed student was back to introducing Glenn.

Taking the podium, John opened his introduction in true rock legend style:

"I've been asked to give a lot of speeches in my career. But I've never been able to start one this way: 'HOW'RE YOU DOING, COLUMBUS?'"

After acknowledging Kerry, the university, and the importance of the upcoming election, Glenn got down to business.

"You know, when you think about it, maybe it's not too surprising that Bruce Springsteen is campaigning for John Kerry.

"After all, they have a lot in common. For one thing, they were both 'Born in the U.S.A.'

"And after his tremendous performance in those three presidential debates, it's also clear that just like Bruce, John Kerry was 'Born to Run.'

"And when it comes to standing up and speaking out on behalf of this nation's working families, there's one more thing John and Bruce have in common.

"They won't give up—and they won't give in. In other words: 'No Retreat... No Surrender.'

"So please join me in welcoming a good man... a great musician... and a true working-class hero... Ladies and gentlemen... The Boss... BRUCE SPRINGSTEEN!"

When the rally concluded, Springsteen said he had a small favor to ask.

Would John be good enough to sign a picture of the two of them shaking hands?

~

Seven years later—in 2011—John unhesitatingly jumped into the middle of a pitched Ohio political battle over "Senate Bill 5," an unprecedented state legislative assault on organized labor that would have stripped Ohio's 400,000 public employees—including teachers, police officers, and firefighters—of their right to strike and bargain collectively. Had the law gone into effect, the public servants who teach our children and keep our communities safe would have been effectively forced to work under whatever terms and conditions school boards and government officials demanded.

Despite championing enormous tax cuts that favored the wealthy and significantly reduced state revenue, Republican Governor John Kasich dubiously insisted that the key to fiscal responsibility lay in restraining spending by the state and local governments. And to do that, he said, it was necessary to enact the draconian SB 5.

Over the strenuous objections of public employee unions and their supporters—whom he warned to "get on the bus or get run over by it"—Kasich managed to ram the controversial legislation through both houses of the Ohio General Assembly.

But there was a wrinkle.

Under the Ohio Constitution, newly enacted state laws are subject to a "citizen's veto" and can be repealed by voters at the ballot box.

It is not, however, an easy process.

In 2011, putting such a referendum on the ballot required backers to obtain 231,149 valid petition signatures from registered voters—a number equal to 6 percent of the total number of voters in the previous (2010) gubernatorial election. Moreover, the signatures had to come from at least forty-four of Ohio's eighty-eight counties.

The umbrella group sponsoring the repeal effort—"We Are Ohio"—stunned nearly everyone by collecting over *1.3 million* signatures, which meant that a referendum on SB 5 was on the November 2011 ballot, where it was designated as "Issue 2." Ohioans wishing to retain SB 5 would vote "yes"; those wanting to repeal it would vote "no."

Having already been recruited by We Are Ohio to be one of its two principal debaters (former Ohio Democratic Congressman Dennis Eckart was the other), I was soon tasked with asking (and perhaps persuading) Senator Glenn to appear in a campaign TV ad.

It was not a hard sell.

After I explained in detail the harm SB 5 would do to public employees—and shared what our internal polling showed was his undiminished credibility with undecided or on-the-fence voters—John quickly agreed to help.

Shooting several different ads for us in the lobby of the Columbus condominium building where he and Annie now lived, Glenn was, as always, believable, persuasive, and effective.

At the time, Issue 2 was far and away the most expensive ballot campaign in Ohio history, with the two sides spending a total of almost $40 million.

On election day, the voters' verdict was overwhelming: Senate Bill 5 was repealed in a 61–39 percent landslide.

At the victory party that night, the campaign's top leaders phoned Senator Glenn at home to thank him for once again stepping into the breach and standing up for Ohio workers. John graciously responded that no thanks were necessary; he simply did what he had always done throughout his career for Ohioans in need of his help.

The Issue 2 campaign would be John's last major political battle.

At the age of ninety, he had run the good race—and had earned the right to spend the rest of his days accepting the accolades of a grateful state and nation.

At a White House ceremony in May 2012, John received the nation's highest civilian honor—the Presidential Medal of Freedom—from President Barack Obama.

But the honor of which John may have been most proud came on June 28, 2016, when Ohio's capital city held a ceremony to change the name of its airport from Port Columbus to John Glenn Columbus International Airport.

The little boy who had begun a lifelong love affair with aviation when his father had taken him to Columbus to see commercial airliners land and take off would now—in the twilight of his life—know that his name would forever be linked to that same airport.

In many ways, it was John's most fitting tribute—and the only honor I'm aware of that made him cry.

Less than six months later—on December 8—John passed away at the age of ninety-five following several weeks of declining health.

Though the news wasn't entirely unexpected, the finality of the moment nevertheless came as a shock. And as I wept, what came to mind were Shakespeare's words from *Romeo and Juliet*:

> And when he shall die,
> Take him and cut him out in little stars,
> And he will make the face of Heaven so fine
> That all the world will be in love with night.

Days later, John became just the ninth person in Ohio history to lie in state in the rotunda of the state capitol, putting him on an august and vanishingly small list that includes Abraham Lincoln.

Thousands of Ohioans—male, female, young, old, titled and workaday, Democrat and Republican—braved the elements on that raw, rainy, and windswept December day to file past John's flag-draped coffin and pay their final respects.

When it was over, a multivehicle funeral procession slowly made its way down High Street from the Statehouse to Mershon Auditorium at Ohio State University, where then–Vice President Joe Biden presided over a moving memorial service for his longtime Senate colleague.

In a statement issued to the news media, I tried to capture what I knew were the feelings not only of John's Senate staff alumni, but of so many Americans from coast to coast:

"Today I join with all Ohioans in mourning the passing of a true giant who always made the rest of us stand a little taller. And I know I speak for patriots everywhere when I say: God speed, John Glenn."

In the spring, after the winter ground thawed, John was laid to rest at Arlington National Cemetery in Washington.

At his behest, a simple inscription is etched into his headstone, modestly describing how he wanted to be remembered:

Fighter Pilot
Astronaut
US Senator

~

On several occasions, John and Annie had both told me—perhaps jokingly, perhaps not—that one of their goals was to reach the age of 100 together.

They almost made it.

But though John fell five years short, Annie—his wife of seventy-three years and the only woman he ever loved or even dated—fulfilled her part of the mission by reaching the century mark by herself before passing away from COVID in 2020. She was laid to rest at Arlington alongside her husband, her soul mate, and her best friend.

The day John died, I wrote an opinion column for *The New York Times* which I titled "*The Last American Hero?*"

I said that while others reflecting on Glenn's one-of-a-kind biography would likely say his death marked the "end of an era," for me, John actually *personified* an era—one that has largely passed from the scene and may never again be recaptured.

It was an age whose values were forged in the Great Depression, tested in history's most bloody war, and expressed at the personal level by the interlocking virtues of modesty, courage, and conviction.

Despite his international celebrity, the ticker-tape parades, and the schools, streets, and facilities named in his honor, John never let any of it go to his head or sought to cash in commercially—which stands in stark contrast to today's more fame-and-clicks-obsessed superstars in politics or popular culture.

John dined with kings, counseled presidents, and signed autographs for athletes, music idols, and movie stars. But he never pulled rank, rarely raised his voice, and remained unfailingly polite and conscious of what he saw as his solemn responsibilities as a national hero and role model.

When he passed away, we lost a man who many say is the last genuine American hero.

Not because others won't do heroic things, but because national heroes aren't easily crowned or even acknowledged in this more cynical age.

In that sense, John Glenn belonged to an earlier and more innocent era—one in which we trusted our national institutions, thought government could accomplish big and important things, still believed politics could be a noble profession, and didn't think ticker-tape parades should be reserved for World Series or Super Bowl champions.

But the last "good" war ended over eighty years ago.

The Cold War is more than thirty years in the past.

America's space program has lost much of its luster.

The clarity with which John saw honor and moral responsibility seems almost quaint today.

And sadly, the time when we could all cheer for the same national hero may now be past.

Chapter Twenty-Three

The Past Isn't Always Prologue, Part I

JOAN DIDION OPENED HER BRILLIANT collection of essays, *The White Album*, with the words "We tell ourselves stories in order to live."

Now well into my seventh decade, I have told the stories in this book not in order to die, but to ensure that when I do, my children and, especially, my grandchildren will know how, why, and toward what ends I spent a good part of my working life.

All five children Vicki and I raised are now adults. Two of them currently hold jobs in public service—and *all* of them vote, follow the news, participate in the political process, and take their responsibilities as citizens very seriously. We are immensely proud of that and of them.

And if our eleven (and counting!) grandchildren and perhaps *their* children can be similarly inspired to understand that democracy is not a spectator sport and that politics and public service need not be dirty words, writing this book will have been more than worth the effort.

I also want younger readers *outside* my family to know that there was once a time not so long ago when politics was neither as coarse in practice nor as apocalyptic in tone or outcome as it often seems today.

John Glenn and Howard Metzenbaum were not saints.

They were human beings who sometimes fell short—and it is neither necessary nor has it been my intent to enlarge them in death beyond what they were in life.

It is enough to remember them as good and decent men who loved this country and devoted the better part of their lives to making it a more perfect union.

For them, politics wasn't a blood sport or a zero-sum game in which opponents were enemies and only one side could win. Above all, as I said in the prologue to this book, they saw compromise not as a moral failing, but as essential to the very survival of our democracy.

If John and Howard were still with us, I believe—no, I *know*—they would be appalled by what our politics have become: tribal, ugly, and so utterly polarized that thoughtful people now reasonably question the future of our republic.

Today, it often seems as if the United States is split into two warring countries, with Democrats and Republicans no longer sharing common goals, a common culture—or even a common reality.

The reasons are myriad:

- Globalization, deindustrialization, and the rise of the information and gig economies that have hollowed out the middle class, robbed those without college degrees of hope, and widened income inequality beyond what it was even in the Gilded Age of the late nineteenth century.
- The advent of ideologically driven cable news networks that make it possible to "choose our news" and cocoon ourselves into ideological silos—along with social media algorithms that narrow our sources of information and steer us into political echo chambers that merely reinforce and never challenge what we want to believe or think we know.
- The surfeit of fringe internet media platforms that are fire hoses of misinformation, disinformation, and conspiracy

theories—the real-world consequences of which were on full display during the COVID pandemic that began in 2020 and killed over one million Americans. Late that year, in an almost miraculously short time, an effective vaccine was developed. But incredibly—as Charles P. Pierce observed in *Esquire* magazine—for the first time in modern American history, there was organized political opposition to the cure for a deadly disease. Never mind that in 1777, George Washington himself—the "father of our country"—ordered the Continental Army to get vaccinated against smallpox: 243 years later, millions of Americans somehow came to regard mask requirements and vaccine mandates as threats to liberty—and to view Dr. Anthony Fauci, perhaps the nation's foremost expert on infectious diseases, as Karl Marx in a lab coat.

- Malign political opportunists—some of whom are Ivy League educated—who surely know better but are morally bereft enough to fan the flames of social and cultural division, undermine faith in our governmental institutions, and encourage their followers to believe that the only legitimate elections are the ones they win.
- And finally, the sense of personal isolation and social disconnectedness that former US Surgeon General Vivek Murthy called an "epidemic of loneliness" that undermines our nation's mental and physical health, reduces our economic productivity, undercuts our collective sense of well-being, and threatens the very underpinnings of our society by making us more prone and susceptible to political polarization.

So where does this toxic stew of loneliness, alienation, hatred, ignorance, and mistrust leave compromise, the lifeblood of democratic government?

Indeed, are compromise and working across the aisle even *desirable* with opponents you've been led to believe are not just wrong, but evil?

For those who have fallen under the spell of Q-Anon or tumbled down other conspiracy theory rabbit holes—or for Donald Trump's Republican acolytes who have come to believe everything they see and hear on extremist right-wing websites and radio shows—the answer is almost certainly "no."

What patriot would be comfortable cooperating with those they believe to be subversives and traitors out to destroy the country and the values we have always held dear? Who but a moral pygmy would give the benefit of the doubt to people they've been told are clandestine pedophiles who sex-traffic children in the basements of neighborhood pizza parlors?

For Democrats, the task is only slightly easier.

How are they supposed to trust or work with those in thrall to a misogynistic, short-fingered vulgarian like Donald Trump who fomented a violent assault on the Capitol, tried to overturn an election, and publicly expressed a desire to "terminate" the Constitution? Someone whose entire career, both in and out of government, has marked him as a narcissistic, kleptocratic huckster who, in the words of Oscar Wilde, "knows the price of everything and the value of nothing?"

Small wonder, then, that a growing number of everyday people tell pollsters that political violence may be necessary—or that a May 2024 Marist poll found that nearly half of all Americans believe a second Civil War is likely in their lifetimes.

I don't pretend to know everything we must do to bridge this divide and get our country back on track.

What I *do* know is that a disturbingly large number of Americans have become increasingly alienated—not just from one another, but also from our economic system and political institutions. And I also know that a persistent sense of helplessness and hopelessness poses a threat to the stability of democracy as we have always known it.

Because I am not a psychologist, I will leave it to mental health professionals to tell us how best to address the "epidemic of loneliness" that is at least partly responsible for our national malaise.

As a retired political professional, I will offer a few thoughts on what we might do in the area of economic and political reform—and will also address in some detail something I believe we absolutely must *not* do if we hope to preserve our democracy.

Let me start on the economic front.

For millions of Americans who once were able to live comfortably middle-class lives by working jobs that did not require advanced training or a college education, the American Dream seems all but dead.

Many of them and their progeny are now working two and even three jobs to make ends meet—and even then, can never seem to get ahead. Socioeconomic mobility as America once knew it—when parents confidently expected their children to have a better life than they did—is, if not buried, very much on life support.

And this depressing state of affairs is occurring even *before* the massive job losses and economic dislocation many observers say artificial intelligence (AI) is all but certain to bring.

A July 2, 2025, *Wall Street Journal* article, for example, quotes Ford Motor Company Chief Executive Jim Farley as saying "Artificial intelligence is going to replace literally half of all white-collar workers in the US."

Anthropic CEO Darlo Amodei goes even further, predicting that "half of all entry-level jobs could disappear in one to five years, resulting in US unemployment of 10 percent to 20 percent." For comparative purposes, the jobless rate during the Great Depression peaked at 25 percent.

If experts like Farley and Amodei are even close to being right, the US economy is about to experience an economic earthquake for which we are totally unprepared—one whose consequences will rival (or even surpass) those of the Industrial Revolution.

Meanwhile, the wealth gap between those at the top and everyone else has become a chasm. The rewards from globalization—which were supposed to make everyone better off—have instead been so unevenly distributed that nearly 62 percent of all the gains in household wealth over the past four years went to the richest 10 percent of the population.

When I graduated from high school in the mid-1960s, the CEO of a Fortune 500 company earned roughly sixteen times more than that company's average employee. According to the *Economic Policy Institute*, today that CEO earns nearly *four hundred times* more than the typical worker.

Indeed, in late 2024 and early 2025 as this book is being written, just three billionaires (Bill Gates, Warren Buffett, and Jeff Bezos) now control more wealth ($248.5 billion) than the bottom half of all Americans *combined* ($245 billion).

Let me repeat that: Three people—*three*—are worth more than 165 million of their fellow Americans put together.

And while American billionaires (let alone millionaires) are proliferating, they often pay a lower federal tax rate than do truck drivers, nurses, and firefighters.

Even worse, because the ultrarich are able to pass down their fantastic wealth in perpetuity to generations yet unborn, we are fast creating a veritable economic aristocracy in which reward is decoupled from work and equality of opportunity often seems like a cynical joke.

For winners of the inheritance lottery, intergenerational wealth for as far as the eye can see—along with the political power and influence that go with it—depends not on talent, ambition, or hard work, but solely on the accident of birth.

In 1776, America's founders rebelled against Great Britain's hereditary aristocracy. It is hard to believe they intended to replace it with a homegrown version.

But the drying up of economic mobility and a widening wealth gap are not the only—or maybe even the primary—reasons so many Americans are steeped in anger and alienation.

There is also a sense of betrayal; a feeling that the Didion-like stories we have been telling ourselves for decades are no longer true.

As conservative University of Notre Dame political science professor Patrick Deneen has put it, it is a story of a society constantly and inevitably getting better through national economic growth and technological advancement; one in which everyday Americans are supposedly richer and far better off than any people who came before us.

But if we are living in the best of all possible worlds, what's not to like? Why are so many people ungrateful?

In reality, millions of Americans *don't* feel better; they feel powerless and vulnerable; trapped in dead-end jobs; stripped of dignity and personal agency by impersonal, faceless, global corporations and government bureaucracies.

These behemoth institutions permeate every aspect of our existence. And they treat us not as human beings, but as replaceable cogs in a ruthless cult of efficiency that seems less concerned with improving our lives or building anything worthwhile than with inventing increasingly clever ways to extract more money, fees, and rule compliance from everyday people.

This, I think, is why so many jobs feel soulless and unfulfilling. It is why so many customers and consumers feel abused by big corporations and big finance—and, perhaps more important, bereft of any real choices.

It is a big reason why nearly 75 percent of Americans tell pollsters they believe the country "is on the wrong track"—and a nationwide Fox News Voter Analysis Poll conducted the week before the 2024 election found that a startling 8 in 10 Americans want substantial change or "complete and total upheaval" in how the country is run.

Upon reflection, it all makes perfect sense.

As Lina Khan, then-chair of the Federal Trade Commission, put it in an August 23, 2024, *New York Times* story, "How people experience power in their day-to-day lives is usually in their economic relationships.... If you're being coerced and bullied in these economic relationships, that's going to affect, really fundamentally, whether you do or don't feel free in our country."

Numerous political leaders have taken notice—including New Right intellectuals like Vice President JD Vance and Republican Senator Josh Hawley, as well as liberal Democratic thinkers like Connecticut Senator Chris Murphy and California Congressman Ro Khanna—who agree that fundamental economic reform is desperately needed.

Where they differ, of course, is on what those reforms should entail.

Conservatives generally call for reduced immigration (legal, as well as illegal), an increase in the US birthrate to pick up the slack, an isolationist foreign policy and a loosening of our traditional alliances such as NATO, an end to free-trade economic policies (often accompanied by universal tariffs), and the wholesale dismantling of the modern administrative state.

Moderates and liberals tend to push for a US government-directed industrial policy, an internationalist foreign policy (and a *strengthening* of traditional alliances), more (legal) immigration, higher taxes on corporations and the wealthy, worker-friendly programs like paid family leave, affordable child and elder care, and the vigorous enforcement of antitrust laws to rein in corporate monopolies.

Though it is impossible to know for sure, I believe the latter proposals are ones that John Glenn and Howard Metzenbaum might wholeheartedly embrace. Indeed, Metzenbaum was an enthusiastic champion of antitrust laws throughout his Senate career, years before it was fashionable.

Interestingly, both the Vance/Hawley wing of the Republican Party and the Murphy/Khanna wing of the Democratic Party are in at least theoretical accord on the need for other economic reforms, such as the creation of more domestic manufacturing jobs, more extensive government investment in non-college postsecondary education, and higher wages for American workers (though they are likely to disagree on the policies needed to achieve those reforms).

Assuming our democracy holds and does not descend into some form of authoritarianism, what is likely to emerge is some combination of these competing visions.

In concept, then, many of these reforms should be doable or at least within the realm of possibility, especially since growing numbers of Democrats and Republicans are coming to believe that significant (and perhaps even fundamental) economic reform is essential to their future electoral success.

Chapter Twenty-Four

The Past Isn't Always Prologue, Part II

SIGNIFICANTLY REFORMING OUR POLITICAL SYSTEM, however, is a different kettle of fish.

As I said earlier, there are many reasons our nation is so politically polarized.

Three of the most prominent are ideologically driven cable TV networks, misinformation-spewing social media platforms, and rank opportunists who see political advantage in fanning the flames of cultural division.

Would that we could wave a magic wand and make these sources of friction disappear.

Unfortunately, there is no such wand—and no realistic hope of putting those genies back in their bottles.

The good news, however, is that most Americans aren't wholly captive to any of these malevolent forces.

Hard-core culture warriors aside, the majority of our citizens are not so politically blinkered as to be totally impervious to facts and reason.

In other words, there is still reason to believe (or, at least, hope) that a working majority of people can be swayed by logical and persuasive arguments aimed at defusing many of the inane "issues" that periodically pop up like whack-a-moles to roil our republic.

The challenge, of course, is how to amplify those countervailing arguments enough to ensure they're heard.

One of my own amplifiers-of-choice is the newspaper op-ed column.

Yes, I am painfully aware that few people read newspapers anymore. But in my experience, insightful op-eds are often passed around among friends, family, and neighbors who may not themselves read newspapers or have subscriptions. Sometimes, a trenchant piece can even "go viral" on social media—and both of these "amplifiers" can exponentially expand the column's original and comparatively puny reach.

Take, for example, what I call the "statue wars" that consumed the country just a few years ago.

In 2020, you may recall, the televised murder of George Floyd by a Minneapolis police officer exposed the continuing reality of racism—and caused most Americans to agree on the need to eliminate our nation's most visible symbols of racial oppression.

But when the call to remove statues and monuments paying homage to leaders of the Confederacy was expanded by liberal activists into a broader attack against memorials to America's founders and other revered icons, comity quickly evaporated.

For some on the left, it seemed morally inconsistent to tear down statues of Confederates who sought to perpetuate slavery while leaving memorials to slave owners like George Washington and Thomas Jefferson intact. And what about monuments to presidents like Andrew Jackson and Ulysses S. Grant, who treated Native Americans with such horrifying brutality?

For some on the right, even raising such questions was seen as another attack on America and her heroes, as well as a ham-handed attempt to erase our nation's history.

But as I suggested in *The Toledo Blade* that summer, applying what I called the "why test" might provide us a way out of the quagmire.

Why was the monument erected in the first place? What was its purpose and what was it intended to honor?

Washington and Jefferson, for example, were commemorated not for owning slaves, but for winning our independence from Great Britain, along with their seminal contributions to founding our constitutional republic.

Monuments to Grant and Jackson weren't erected to celebrate their mistreatment of Native Americans, but to extol Grant for winning the Civil War and preserving our union—and to honor Jackson for his role in winning the War of 1812 and for his presidential anti-nullification declaration that equated secession with treason.

Similarly, Franklin D. Roosevelt earned his memorial in Washington for pulling our country out of the Great Depression and defeating the Nazis in World War II, not for consigning Japanese Americans to internment camps.

I was not suggesting that we excuse or deny anyone's mistakes. Only that we recognize that all human beings are flawed—and that these men, like all of us, were products of their times.

If monuments are reserved only for the perfect, surely there will be no monuments at all.

But if a "why" test would leave a majority of our statues up, it would also provide a logically consistent rationale for taking those of Confederate leaders down.

Unlike memorials to Washington, Jefferson, or Grant, monuments to Jefferson Davis, Robert E. Lee, and "Stonewall" Jackson celebrate not their pursuit of a shared national purpose, but their willingness to destroy the nation itself in order to preserve the right of white Americans to own Black Americans, whom they could beat, rape, and even murder at will.

In short, Confederate generals and politicians took up arms against the United States—a textbook definition of treason that directly caused the deaths of nearly 700,000 Americans, double the toll of World War II, and more than in all our nation's other wars put together.

Moreover—and perhaps most revealingly with respect to their purpose—most Confederate monuments were not erected immediately after the Civil War as displays of heritage and remembrance, but many decades later as symbols of southern defiance.

The first surge came in the late 1890s and early 1900s in celebration of the South's repudiation of Reconstruction and its imposition of Jim Crow laws.

A second spike occurred in the 1950s and '60s as part of the South's "massive resistance" response to court-ordered school desegregation and the enactment of federal civil rights and voting rights laws.

There is a big difference, I wrote, between remembering our history and romanticizing or whitewashing it.

Relocating Confederate statues to museums or privately maintained parks is one thing.

Granting them a place of honor in our public squares is something else again.

Monuments intended to further the ideals of white supremacy are not worthy of veneration.

And surely, we can all agree that traitors don't belong on pedestals.

That op-ed generated as much reaction as any I've ever written. It was circulated online by conservatives and liberals alike—and unlike some of my other columns, I can't remember reading a single negative comment.

Many readers said it caused them to consider the issue in a different and less political way. Others thanked me for bringing common sense to a contentious issue.

Though a few die-hard Confederate apologists or white supremacists doubtlessly took umbrage, the vast majority saw it as a good faith effort both to find common ground and to lower our nation's political temperature.

I'm not so naive, of course, to think that all—or even most—hot-button issues can be resolved or wrestled to the ground via thoughtful, well-meaning columns or commentators.

But if enough Americans are willing to look for common ground when contentious subjects arise, perhaps we can at least reduce the number of issues that push partisans to the barricades.

And that would be a welcome start.

Chapter Twenty-Five

The Past Isn't Always Prologue, Part III

DIMINISHING THE DISAPPOINTMENT AND EVEN anger many Americans have toward our political system will require far-reaching reforms—some of which probably aren't possible to implement, at least at the present moment.

Take, for example, the commonly heard lament that "voting doesn't matter."

In truth, it often doesn't—if "matter" is defined as government actually doing what a majority of voters wants it to.

And that is partly attributable to a series of antimajoritarian compromises our forefathers made nearly 250 years ago as they struggled to create a country.

Let me explain.

The Archaic Compromises That Stifle Majority Rule

In the late 1700s when the founders junked the Articles of Confederation and sought to create a constitutional republic, a dispute arose—but *not* between highly populated "big states" and lightly populated "small states." The split was between North and South.

Because Southern states had far more slaves than slave owners, the latter feared—at a time when only white men who owned property could cast ballots—being perpetually outvoted by non–slave owners in the Northern states.

Enter three major compromises:

a. *Counting slaves as three-fifths of a person.* This, of course, would give Southern states a larger number of seats in the House of Representatives (where representation is based solely on population) than they would get if only "free" people were counted. But since slaves were legally defined as property and not as actual people, counting them as three-fifths of a person would give white property owners the political outcome they sought without upsetting the legal applecart.
b. *Giving every state two Senate seats regardless of population.*
c. *Choosing presidents via an "Electoral College,"* rather than through the popular vote. Since the number of electoral votes each state has is equal to its total number of House and Senate seats, this, too, enhanced the political power of Southern states and slave owners.

Though slavery is long gone, two of these three "compromises" (the Electoral College and allotting two senators per state) remain very much with us—and together make a mockery of majority rule, the one-person-one-vote principle, and the broadly held conviction that no citizen's vote should count more than that of any other citizen.

Consider presidential elections, for instance. Though Democratic candidates won more popular votes than Republican candidates in seven of the last nine presidential elections (1992, 1996, 2000, 2008, 2012, 2016, and 2020), Republicans nevertheless captured the presidency in two of those contests (2000 and 2016) because of the Electoral College.

In every other election we have in this country—from Congress to City Hall to dogcatcher—the person with the most votes wins. Why do we still insist on something different when choosing a president?

The standard and often knee-jerk justification for keeping the Electoral College is that without it, "big" states like California or New York would have a larger say in picking presidents than sparsely populated states like Wyoming or Rhode Island.

But think about that for a minute.

The only reason *any* state has any power at all is because of the Electoral College.

Without it, every citizen's vote would count exactly the same as every other citizen's, regardless of where they happen to live.

To put a finer (and bipartisan) point on it, why should the vote of a Republican in Massachusetts matter less than one cast by a Republican in Idaho? Why should the vote of a Democrat in Utah be more impactful than the vote of a Democrat in Illinois?

But the problem isn't limited to the question of who occupies the White House.

Take the issue of reproductive rights.

Despite polls showing that nearly 70 percent of Americans favored keeping the abortion standards of *Roe v. Wade*, the Supreme Court overturned it in 2022 by a 6–3 vote.

Four of those six justices—that is, the majority of the majority that overturned *Roe*—were appointed by two presidents who lost the popular vote, but won the office via the Electoral College. One of them—Donald Trump—was able to appoint *three* of those four justices in his first term as president, despite having lost the 2016 popular vote by more than three million votes.

And *all* of those justices were confirmed by an unrepresentative Senate in which the 42 million Americans who live in California get two senators, while the 1.7 million people who live in the Dakotas get four.

In short, archaic compromises reached more than two centuries ago—even if charitably and alternatively interpreted as good faith attempts to protect minority factions and prevent a "tyranny of the majority"—have devolved into an evisceration of majority rule and, worse yet, a functional tyranny of the *minority.*

Small wonder so many Americans feel frustrated and think their votes don't matter.

Admittedly, there may not be a practical alternative to every state having two US senators—or perhaps I'm just not smart enough to know what it is.

But with respect to the Electoral College, an alternative is obvious: Simply treat presidential elections the same way we treat every other election and declare that the person getting the most votes is the winner.

Alas, what's obvious isn't always doable. Especially here, since discarding the Electoral College would mean amending the Constitution which, while always difficult, in this case would be next to impossible.

As noted earlier, constitutional amendments must be approved by two-thirds of the members in both houses of Congress—and then ratified by three-quarters of the states. That's a high bar—and why, following the adoption of the Bill of Rights, the Constitution has been amended just seventeen times since 1791.

Needless to say, eliminating the Electoral College via a constitutional amendment is unlikely to happen. Not only because small states very much enjoy the outsized power it gives them—but also because the current arrangement redounds to the benefit of one of America's two major political parties.

How many Republicans would willingly jettison something that can (and does) hand them the presidency or appointments to the Supreme Court even if they get fewer popular votes than their opponents?

But if getting rid of the Electoral College isn't in the cards anytime soon, there are two other reforms we *can* make to reduce the degree of antimajoritarianism in our political system.

Happily, neither would require a constitutional amendment.

Two Achievable Political Reforms

One is abolishing the Senate filibuster—and the other is eliminating gerrymandering in drawing the lines of congressional (and state legislative) districts.

Let me address the filibuster first.

For those only vaguely familiar with the term, a filibuster is a tactic used by a minority of senators to delay or block a vote from taking place by preventing the debate on whatever is at issue from ending. The only way to break a filibuster and end debate is by invoking "cloture"—which today requires the approval of sixty senators.

Absent cloture, in other words, a single senator can stall a vote indefinitely and prevent his or her other 99 colleagues from passing a piece of legislation.

Though it is nowhere mentioned in the Constitution, the Senate filibuster has existed from the nation's earliest days (the House does not permit unlimited debate), but historically was used sparingly, most notably against civil rights legislation in the 1950s and '60s. Only in more recent years has the filibuster been routinely used to prevent passage of any bill or law opposed by a minority of senators.

Though the original purpose of the filibuster was to protect minority points of view—and it is sometimes defended today as a means of ensuring "bipartisanship" in the passage of laws—its abuse has, in reality, led to legislative paralysis.

Want to know why the 118th Congress—which ended in January 2025—was the least productive Congress since 1860, when America was on the eve of civil war? One reason is that today, thanks to the abuse of the filibuster, nothing of substance can pass in the Senate with a simple majority of 51 votes. Even routine legislation needs a *supermajority* of at least 60 votes.

We know this isn't what the founders who wrote our Constitution intended—and not only because Alexander Hamilton warned against supermajority strictures in *Federalist Paper No. 22*.

We also know it because the Constitution they wrote identifies just five situations in which a supermajority is required: the override of presidential vetoes, impeachments, and the expulsion of members of Congress (all in Article I); the ratification of treaties (in Article II); and the approval of constitutional amendments (in Article V).

For everything else, only a simple majority was necessary for action which, in modern times, translates into 51 votes in the Senate and 218 in the House of Representatives.

Had the founders believed passage of *legislation* should require a supermajority, they surely would have said so.

For supporters of majority rule who believe the will of the people should be respected, the good news is that because the filibuster is merely one of the Senate's "standing rules" and isn't in the Constitution, it can be consigned to the dustbin of history if just 51 senators vote to eliminate it.

But won't discarding the filibuster mean that both parties, Democrats and Republicans alike, would no longer be able to bottle up legislation they oppose? Would it not increase the possibility that truly horrendous laws might be passed?

Yes, it would—something I know is top of mind for Democrats in 2025 as Donald Trump embarks on another term as president buoyed by a Republican-controlled Congress.

But in my view, those outcomes and the risk they pose are worth enduring if it means ending congressional paralysis and ridding the country of one of its most glaring vestiges of antimajoritarianism.

Please do not misunderstand me. One of the best and most brilliant things about the constitutional republic designed by James Madison and his fellow framers was its protection of minority rights.

But if they didn't see the filibuster as necessary to the protection of those rights, why should we?

And whatever our partisan political affiliation, I hope we can corporately agree there is a big difference between protecting minority rights and letting minorities run roughshod over the majority.

Moreover, elections are *supposed* to have consequences.

If voters elect a president and put that president's party in charge of Congress, they have a right to expect that those officeholders will be able to enact the policies and programs they promised to pursue. If voters don't like the outcome, they are free to oust the politicians and party responsible in the next election.

In the meantime, let's stop the losers from obstructing the winners. Let's make Congress productive again, and seize the opportunity to restore a measure of faith in our system. And let us, at long last, show the American people that their votes actually *do* matter.

Ending the filibuster would be a step toward all of those things.

A second major reform we can make is to stop the practice of gerrymandering.

For those who may have only a foggy understanding of the term, gerrymandering is drawing legislative maps or districts that unfairly favor one political party over another.

It occurs during the process of "political redistricting"—a once-every-ten-years exercise in which the political boundaries that demarcate congressional and state legislative districts are redrawn to reflect population shifts identified in the national census.

Though the Constitution requires redistricting only once every ten years, in 2025 a number of states are now embroiled in a mid-decade gerrymandering arms race. President Trump successfully urged Texas to redraw its lines once again to give Republicans five new seats in the House of Representatives ahead of the 2026 midterm elections. California responded by threatening to gerrymander its own congressional map mid-decade to increase its number of Democratic House seats. Several other states, both red and blue, have now joined the partisan fray and entered the gerrymandering sweepstakes. As this book is being written, the ultimate outcome is unclear.

While the mechanisms for redistricting vary from state to state, in virtually every case where politicians are in charge of the process, lines are drawn in ways that overtly favor Republicans or Democrats, depending on which party is holding the pencil.

Though gerrymandering has been practiced since the earliest days of the republic, what is new is how much more sophisticated the stratagem has become.

Before computers and other high-tech gadgetry, gerrymandering was imprecise and districts often turned out to be much more competitive than the parties intended. Today, however, it is possible to determine street by street and even house by house exactly who is likely to vote how.

The result is districts so solidly either Republican or Democratic that the outcome of a general election is almost a foregone conclusion before it even takes place.

How bad is it? In 2024, according to the authoritative *Cook Political Report*, only about 36 congressional races nationwide (out of a total of 435) were competitive and just 24 were rated as "toss-ups." In Ohio, the nonpartisan Brennan Center for Justice says that about 77 percent of the state's population lives in districts where elections for state representative are not competitive.

There are two reasons gerrymandering is so pernicious.

First, it is irredeemably antimajoritarian. By definition, it ensures that some votes (and voters) count more than others by artificially inflating the strength of one party while artificially diluting the strength of the other.

How gerrymandering accomplishes this is easy to understand.

The party in charge of mapmaking draws what are often weirdly shaped districts designed and intended to pack as many of the other party's voters into as few districts as possible, thus leaving the lion's share to be won by the party controlling the process.

One need look no further than my home state of Ohio to see how grossly unfair this is.

Here—in a state where, over the past ten years, Republican candidates have captured just 54 percent of the vote for congressional candidates—

Ohio's 15-member delegation to the House of Representatives is composed of 10 Republicans and 5 Democrats.

Similarly, of the 99 members of the Ohio House, 65 are Republican and 34 are Democrats.

In the 33-member state Senate, the imbalance is even worse: 24 seats are held by the Republicans and just 9 by Democrats.

Equally absurd numbers abound—but in reverse—in states where Democrats control the map-drawing process.

Gerrymandering's blatant unfairness and scorn for the will of the voters would be reasons enough to end it.

But in my view, there's something else that makes it even more deleterious.

By discouraging compromise and rewarding intransigence, gerrymandering poisons our politics by perpetuating (and even exacerbating) the polarization that threatens our democracy.

Recall that in gerrymandered districts that heavily favor either Democrats or Republicans, winners of a general election are almost never in doubt. For incumbents, danger lurks only in the next primary election.

And since primary election outcomes are largely determined by party activists, Republicans naturally fear being attacked from "the right," while Democrats are afraid of being attacked from "the left." In such situations, there is virtually no political incentive for officeholders from either party to compromise or cooperate with the "other side."

In fact, the exact *opposite* is true: Incumbents in gerrymandered districts can best maximize their political longevity by remaining ideologically pure and *refusing* to cooperate with legislators from the opposite party. This will satisfy their party's base and greatly diminish the prospect of drawing a challenger in the next primary election.

If I could rub a lamp and summon a genie to grant me one political wish that might lessen tensions, reduce polarization, and short-circuit the hyper-partisanship in our country, I would ask for an end to gerrymandering.

Consider:

If rather than being drawn to favor one party over the other, districts were instead created to contain (insofar as law and practicality allow), *equal* numbers of Democrats and Republicans, the political dynamic would suddenly reverse to *disfavor* obstinacy and *favor* compromise.

Why? Because in order to be elected, GOP candidates would need votes from Democrats, and Democratic candidates would have to earn votes from Republicans.

This would give *both* parties an incentive to work together—and candidates would soon learn that being rigid, unyielding, or excessively ideological is a surefire ticket to Loserville.

But regardless of how much sense a reform like this might make, upending gerrymandering won't be easy—and it can't be done simply by passing a federal law.

In America, elections are not run by the federal government; they're administered by the fifty states, which means fifty different sets of rules, laws, and practices.

In other words, there are no federal standards that apply to partisan gerrymandering.

The US Supreme Court reaffirmed this regrettable reality in 2019 when, in a case from North Carolina, it ruled that gerrymandering for partisan political purposes is outside the scope of federal law.

Not that all the justices themselves are necessarily happy about it. As former Justice Anthony Kennedy succinctly put it: "It is unfortunate that when it comes to apportionment, we are in the business of rigging elections."

But the lack of federal jurisdiction doesn't make us powerless or forever condemn us to suffer gerrymandering.

It only means that getting rid of it will take longer because we'll have to wage the battle state by state.

Four states—Arizona, California, Colorado, and Michigan—have already taken the plunge and created independent, nonpartisan processes for drawing legislative districts.

In 2024, Ohio had a chance to join their ranks by passing "Issue 1"—an amendment to the Ohio constitution that would have taken mapmaking away from Statehouse politicians and given it to a fifteen-member independent commission composed of five Republicans, five Democrats, and five Independents, all appointed by a panel of retired judges. Politicians and lobbyists would be banned from serving on the commission.

The proposal was written and sponsored by a bipartisan coalition called "Citizens, Not Politicians" led by two former state Supreme Court justices, one of whom is a former chief justice and a Republican.

Because Ohio is among the most gerrymandered states in the nation—and with polls uniformly showing strong bipartisan support for ending the practice—there was every reason to believe Issue 1 would pass handily.

Despite a hopeful beginning—in which the coalition was able to gather nearly 60 percent more voter signatures than necessary to get it on the ballot—Issue 1 ultimately became a pitched, partisan battle. For Republicans who benefited from gerrymandering, no tactic was too extreme and no ruse was too odious if it meant preserving their prerogative to draw self-serving maps.

With the help of a secretary of state who does not embarrass easily, they even stooped to writing false and misleading ballot language suggesting that Issue 1 would somehow "require gerrymandering to continue"—the *exact opposite* of the proposal's intent.

Ironically, this subterfuge probably ensured that many "no" voters mistakenly thought they actually were casting ballots *against* gerrymandering. Or as Alex Triantafilou, the chairman of the Ohio Republican Party, smugly put it in a January 2025 speech to the Sandusky County GOP, "confusing Ohioans was not such a bad strategy."

In late October, Republicans also cleverly enlisted the support of their presidential candidate, Donald Trump, who cut a television ad implying that the bipartisan anti-gerrymandering effort was some kind of nefarious Democratic plot and imploring his supporters to vote "no." For low-information voters who typically show up only in presidential election years (and likely were less familiar with what the ballot fight was all about), Trump's opposition by itself may have been enough to sink the proposal.

In any event, the Republicans' machinations worked. Issue 1 was defeated and, at least for now, gerrymandering will continue in Ohio.

But I remain optimistic. Both here in Ohio and across the country, I believe most people want a fair map-drawing process that doesn't rig the outcome of elections before they're held—and that allows voters to pick their legislators, not one that allows legislators to pick their voters.

It may take a while. But sooner or later, I believe voters will see through the smoke and mirrors employed by self-seeking politicians. Sooner or later, they will demand commonsense reform. And sooner or later, I believe they will put an end to gerrymandering once and for all.

Chapter Twenty-Six

The Past Isn't Always Prologue, Part IV

IN THE PREVIOUS TWO CHAPTERS, I've outlined a few economic and political reforms I believe might reduce the tribalism, division, and alienation that are wracking our country.

In this final chapter, I want to end not with a "do" but with a "don't"—something that I believe we must steer clear of if we want to avoid throwing even more sparks into the culture war powder keg that is already threatening to explode our democracy.

In my view—a view that I know Senators Glenn and Metzenbaum emphatically shared—it would be a catastrophic mistake to turn our collective back on the separation of church and state our founders so wisely insisted upon. Nothing good can possibly come from injecting religion even more deeply into the combustible mix of contemporary politics.

Please do not misunderstand me.

I am in no way antireligion.

In my personal life, I earned a degree from a church-affiliated college and have been an ordained elder in the Presbyterian Church for over thirty years.

In my professional life, I have proudly worked for practicing Christians like John Glenn and practicing Jews like Howard Metzenbaum—and like so many other Americans, I know how comforting faith can be in times of trouble or despair.

But I also know that at a time when our country has more religious diversity than ever before, few things could be more dangerous than indulging the idea that the United States of America was founded as a "Christian nation"—and that we should rewrite our laws to reinforce that fallacy.

Contrary to those who glibly preach the gospel of Christian Nationalism, the idea that America was designed to be "Christian" ignores the historical record and would be complete anathema to those who wrote the US Constitution.

While it is true that most of our founders were grounded in the European Christian tradition, they were at least equally influenced by the rationalism of the Enlightenment.

And a key tenet of the latter was the importance of creating separate spheres for faith and reason in worldly affairs.

Mark Twain is said to have observed that "it ain't what you don't know that gets you into trouble. It's what you know for sure that just ain't so."

Nowhere is that more evident than in what many Americans think *they know for sure* about the religious beliefs of our nation's forefathers.

Despite what these benighted folks may have always believed, it is an indisputable fact that only *some* of our Founding Fathers, such as Samuel Adams, Patrick Henry, and John Jay, were Christians.

A few, like Ethan Allen and Thomas Paine, were either atheists or close enough to be credibly accused.

Many more, including Thomas Jefferson, Benjamin Franklin, George Washington, James Madison, and James Monroe, are probably best described as Deists or, perhaps more precisely, theistic rationalists.

But whatever their personal religious views, there is absolutely no doubt about the kind of republic they sought to create.

In 1789—after robust debate in Philadelphia over whether to include the words—the founders adopted a Constitution that makes no reference to "God," "Jesus," or "the Bible."

Indeed, religious tests for holding public office are *specifically forbidden* under Article VI.

In 1797, the Senate—which was then still chock-full of Founding Fathers—unanimously ratified the Treaty of Tripoli (negotiated under our first president and signed by our second), which flatly declared that "*the Government of the United States of America is not in any sense founded on the Christian religion.*"

It is hard to imagine a more dispositive statement.

Nor can it come as a surprise to those who know what our founders actually believed about the dangers of intertwining church and state.

In 1785, for example—four years before becoming the Constitution's chief architect—James Madison memorably described the danger of government support of religion in any form in his *Memorial and Remonstrance against Religious Assessments*:

> During almost fifteen centuries has the legal establishment of Christianity been on trial. What have been its fruits? More or less in all places, pride and indolence in the Clergy, ignorance and servility in the laity, in both, superstition, bigotry and persecution.

And if all of this weren't enough, Thomas Jefferson—the nation's third president and author of the Declaration of Independence—famously coined the term "wall of separation" in his 1802 *letter to the Danbury Baptist Association* as he sought to explain how he and his fellow founders viewed the proper interplay between church and state.

Though there have been periodic eruptions of theocratic fervor throughout our nation's history, the conviction that our government and its laws must be secular and nonsectarian has remained more or less intact for well over two hundred years.

Indeed, when Democrats nominated a Roman Catholic for president in 1960, John F. Kennedy doubted he could win if he didn't stress his resolve to separate his religious beliefs from the conduct of his official duties.

His doubt was well founded; the fear that a Catholic would "take orders from the Pope" was at least partially responsible for Al Smith's defeat in 1928, the only other time a person of that faith had previously been nominated for president by a major party.

In fact, many historians believe Kennedy would have suffered the same fate had he not given a speech to the *Greater Houston Ministerial Association* a few weeks before the election in which he emphatically stated, "I am not the Catholic candidate for President; I am the Democratic candidate for President who happens also to be a Catholic."

After declaring "I believe in an America where the separation of church and state is absolute," Kennedy then pledged never to allow his religious convictions to dictate his public policy positions.

But as I pointed out in op-ed columns for *The Columbus Dispatch* in 2022 and the *Abilene Reporter-News* in 2023, the separation of church and state has come under increasing assault in recent years; ironically, most often by self-described "conservatives" who rarely miss a chance to trumpet their fidelity to the Constitution.

Some, like former Trump cabinet member Secretary Ben Carson, have forthrightly declared Muslims unfit to serve as president.

Equally worrisome, a large number of voters tell pollsters they won't vote for anyone who isn't a Christian—or for candidates who fail to support laws based on Christian doctrine.

It is supremely ironic that the religious issue has now come full circle: sixty-four years ago, many Americans would only vote for a candidate who pledged *not* to let his religious beliefs determine his policy positions; six decades later, many voters will only support candidates who pledge *the exact opposite.*

We are moving in a dangerous direction.

In 2023, the first question Senator Lindsey Graham (R-SC) asked of Supreme Court nominee Ketanji Brown Jackson during her confirmation hearing was, "What faith are you? On a scale of 1–10, how faithful would you say you are in terms of religion?"

It is one thing to question candidates about their value systems and moral compasses. It is quite another to contravene Article VI of the Constitution by imposing *de facto* religious tests for public office. Even if, I might add, such tests are imposed *indirectly* by voters.

At the very least, perhaps we can all agree that those who flout Article VI because they don't believe it belongs in our Constitution should at least be honest enough to actively and openly seek its repeal.

So how *should* we approach the issue of politics and religion?

First, it is important to remember that because politics is often about values—and because many people derive their values from their religious beliefs—it is all but impossible to completely separate the two.

Yet who among us can claim infallibility or to have a monopoly on truth?

Getting along in a pluralistic society requires that while all faiths are respected, none is enshrined—officially or otherwise—in our laws or our government.

This is not to deny the tension that exists—and that we have struggled to navigate throughout our history—between the "establishment" and "free exercise" clauses of the First Amendment. It is merely to suggest that while believers must always be free to worship as they choose, they must never be permitted to impose their beliefs on others or to deny them, for sectarian reasons, the basic rights we all enjoy as citizens.

Second, we must recognize that there is nothing wrong with people of faith offering counsel to government leaders. In fact, there is much to commend it.

But when they do, it is incumbent upon them to recognize the critical distinction that exists between offering advice and counsel—and asserting that this or that political position is the "will of God."

God's will does not lend itself to compromise.

And yet we know that compromise—especially on contentious, legislative issues—is indispensable to a functioning democracy.

In my view, this means that with respect to moral issues on which the public is deeply divided (like, say, Prohibition in the 1920s or abortion today), religious believers should focus more on changing minds than on changing laws. And that, in turn, means they should restrict their appeal to the conscience of the individual, not the coercive power of the state.

Third, it is also essential that believers resist the temptation to judge a candidate's fitness for office by where or how often they worship—or even by whether they believe or disbelieve.

It is simply too slippery a slope—as our nation's history amply demonstrates.

In past eras, the targets of discrimination and political exclusion were Jews and Catholics—and in colonial Virginia, even Baptists.

Today's targets might be Muslims, Mormons, or athcists.

Tomorrow's targets could be... who knows?

The only fail-safe way to ensure that *no one* becomes a target—and that the blessings of liberty are shared by all—is to insist not that our leaders pledge to a particular faith, but that they pledge to keep faith with the Constitution of the United States.

Finally, it is important to emphasize that strictly separating church and state does *not* require sublimating moral principles in the exercise of political power. On the contrary; morality should *always* inform and be part of our political calculus.

Separation merely requires us to recognize that only through civility, tolerance, and a willingness to respect one another on matters of conscience can we adhere to the Constitution—and keep our country safe for both democracy and diversity.

A Final Thought

IN 2025 AS THIS BOOK is being written, American democracy is under enormous stress and beset by a host of seemingly intractable problems: a population that appears hopelessly divided and increasingly angry . . . cable television networks and social media platforms that amplify our discord and make it difficult for us to agree on even the most basic of facts . . . endless culture wars that poison our politics, split our families, and pit neighbor against neighbor . . . fraying economic and political systems that are losing support and need transformational reforms that often seem beyond our capacity to effectuate.

And all of this was true even *before* Donald Trump was elected president again in 2024, vowing to exact legal revenge against his opponents, use military force against his critics, undo our international alliances, and impose an authoritarian style of governance the US has never experienced in its nearly 250-year history.

Our situation is undeniably fraught.

But perhaps because I spent a good portion of my career working with towering figures like John Glenn and Howard Metzenbaum—and saw firsthand what monumental achievements great leaders can make us capable of—I remain optimistic.

America has faced difficult days and seemingly insurmountable challenges before—slavery, pandemics, a Great Depression, two world wars, a Cold War, and even a Civil War.

But over and over—against the odds—we have risen to the challenge and met the moment. For two and a half centuries, we somehow have always found a way not just to muddle through and survive, but to emerge better and stronger than we were before.

And that history—*our* history—proves that we need not rely on magical thinking nor depend, like Dr. Samuel Johnson's twice-married gentleman, on the triumph of hope over experience.

On the contrary. We can believe in America precisely *because* of our experience.

And what our experience tells us is that even in days of doubt and eras of existential challenge, America's best days have always proved to be ahead of us and never behind us.

Perhaps that is reason enough to believe that for us as Americans, the past truly *can* be prologue.

So to paraphrase a young and inspirational president who galvanized my own generation, let us go forth with courage and conviction, united in our resolve to heal this land we love—asking His blessing and His help—but knowing that here on earth, God's work must truly be our own.

About John Glenn

JOHN HERSCHEL GLENN JR. WAS born in Cambridge, Ohio, on July 18, 1921, and was raised in nearby New Concord. A twenty-three-year veteran of the US Marine Corps, he fought in World War II and Korea, flying 149 combat missions and winning six Distinguished Flying Crosses and eighteen Air Medals. As a test pilot, he flew the first supersonic transcontinental flight across the US in 1957. Selected as one of the original seven Mercury astronauts, Glenn became the first American to orbit the earth, on February 20, 1962, aboard *Friendship 7*. His subsequent ticker-tape parade in New York City saw more tons of confetti dropped than in any other parade before or since. He was married for seventy-three years to his childhood sweetheart, Annie (Castor), and raised two children, Dave and Lyn.

Following his retirement from the Marine Corps in 1965, Glenn worked in the private sector at soft-drink company Royal Crown, serving as a corporate vice president and president of the company's international division.

After two abortive bids for the US Senate in 1964 (which ended after a bathtub fall caused an inner ear injury) and 1970 (when he lost in the Democratic primary), Glenn won a Senate seat in 1974—and voters returned him to office three more times, making him the only elected four-term Senator in Ohio history.

In the Senate he was a member of the Foreign Relations, Armed Services, Intelligence, Special Committee on Aging, and Governmental Affairs Committees, serving as chairman of the latter from 1987 to 1995.

Among his legislative achievements, the three of which he was most proud were the Nuclear Non-Proliferation Act of 1978 (which sought to slow the spread of nuclear weapons around the planet), the Inspector General Act of 1978 (designed to find and reduce waste and fraud in federal agencies and departments), and the 1995 Congressional Accountability Act (which requires Congress to abide by the same civil rights, labor, and workplace safety laws as those imposed on private enterprise).

He returned to space in 1998 aboard Space Shuttle *Discovery* and thus became both the first and the oldest American to orbit the earth. He was awarded the Presidential Medal of Freedom in 2012.

John Glenn passed away in Columbus on December 8, 2016, at the age of ninety-five. He is buried in Arlington National Cemetery.

About Howard Metzenbaum

HOWARD MORTON METZENBAUM WAS BORN on June 4, 1917, in Cleveland. After receiving undergraduate and law degrees from Ohio State University, he provided legal representation for labor unions and had a successful business career in real estate and airport parking lot development. He and his wife, Shirley (Turoff), were married for sixty-one years and raised four daughters: Barbara, Susan, Shelley, and Amy.

Metzenbaum served two terms in the Ohio House of Representatives and one term in the Ohio Senate before running for the US Senate in 1970, winning the nomination in a Democratic primary but losing the general election that fall. In 1974, he lost the nomination in a Democratic primary, but he won a Senate seat in 1976, ousting Republican Robert Taft Jr. He was reelected twice—in 1982 and 1988—before deciding not to seek a fourth term in 1994.

In the Senate, he was best known for his service on the Labor and Judiciary Committees, and he authored or was the primary sponsor of forty-two different laws.

Perhaps his proudest achievements were the Worker Adjustment and Retraining Notification Act of 1988 (which requires companies employing 100 or more people to give sixty days' notice before closing a plant or factory), the Brady Law of 1993 (which establishes a waiting period for handgun purchases), the Nutrition Labeling and Education Act of 1990 (which requires food manufacturers to list nutrition facts and understandable claims about their products), and the Metzenbaum Multiethnic Placement Act of 1994 (which prohibits federally subsidized adoption agencies from denying child placement on grounds of race or ethnicity). He also reveled in his unofficial nickname of "Senator No" for his willingness to block controversial presidential appointments and the passage of complex legislation or amendments that he believed were insufficiently vetted or being rushed through the Senate at the behest of special interests.

Upon his retirement from the Senate in 1995, Metzenbaum served as chairman of the Consumer Federation of America. He passed away in Aventura, Florida, on March 12, 2008, at the age of ninety and is buried in Cleveland Heights, Ohio. In 1998, the Old Federal Building and Post Office in downtown Cleveland was renamed the Howard M. Metzenbaum United States Courthouse.

A Note on Methods and Sources

THIS BOOK IS A MEMOIR and is based on memory and material I have retained over the years, including speech drafts and contemporaneous notes I made after meetings, phone calls, and political events. I have used direct quotes only when I either vividly remember or made a note of what was said. In all other cases, I have used paraphrase to capture the essence and meaning of what was expressed.

I have undertaken much fact-checking, both online and otherwise, to ensure that dates, statistics, and things stated as fact are accurate. And I have enormously benefited from the help and assistance of several longtime friends and colleagues, some of whom were in the political arena in one capacity or another during the years covered in this book. Among these invaluable (but, happily for me, unpaid) research assistants are Mike Curtin, Eric Schnurer, Bob Shrum, and Emily Ackerman. They identified several mistakes in early drafts, and their suggestions and edits were both welcome and constructive. Any responsibility for errors, of course, is mine alone.

The stories I have told and the anecdotes I have related in these pages are all true, even if some of them strain credulity. That they *are* true only reinforces my long-held conviction that in politics—perhaps more than in any other field of endeavor—truth is, indeed, often stranger than fiction.

I cared for the candidates and officeholders whose stories are told in this book, and always gave them and their campaigns my very best efforts. Whether they won or lost, I believed in them—and in their commitment to the common good.

Acknowledgments

NEITHER THIS BOOK NOR MY career in politics would have been possible without John Glenn. He gave me my first job on Capitol Hill and took chances on me over and over again. As one of the nation's best-known US senators, he could have had his pick of experienced political speechwriters but chose to hire a complete unknown. When he needed a press secretary after his presidential campaign ended, he took a flyer on an inexperienced wannabe with no credentials. And when he decided to seek an unprecedented fourth term as US senator from Ohio, he turned to me even though I had never managed a campaign. I like to think I rose to those occasions and that John never regretted putting his faith in me. But few would have blamed him had he put his faith elsewhere—and it is no exaggeration to say he's largely responsible for nearly everything I've accomplished professionally. For me, John Glenn was more than just a national hero; he was and always will be my personal hero as well.

I also want to acknowledge the many people I worked with in John's Senate office for nearly two decades. The late Bill White, Kathy Bovard, and the late Ed Furtek were all wonderful chiefs of staff. Ed became my closest friend in Washington and I still miss him immensely. Martha DiSario was my deputy press secretary and one of the best publicists I've ever known.

Mary Jane Veno, who was extraordinarily close to the senator and had his trust, always kept things interesting, and Eileen Bradner, Diane Lifsey, Kathy Connolly, Susan Carnohan, Pat Buckheit, Lorraine Lewis, Brian Dettlebach, and Ron Grimes did yeoman's work on legislative issues. Carl Ford was John's foreign policy adviser *extraordinaire,* and Len Weiss, who headed the staff of John's Governmental Affairs Committee, was a fount of often complicated but always important legislative initiatives. Space alone prevents me from naming other Glenn staffers who deserve to be acknowledged. On John's 1984 presidential campaign, my fellow speechwriters Eric Schnurer and Dennis Fitzgibbons were dedicated professionals who made that two-year grind tolerable and frequently fun.

I cherish the year I spent working for Howard Metzenbaum, Ohio's other US senator during the 1970s and '80s, and will always be grateful that he asked John to "loan" me to his 1988 reelection effort. It was one of the best-run campaigns I've ever been a part of, and it was thanks to Howard that I learned the political potency of economic populism. Contrary to his frequently dour public persona, Metzenbaum always treated me with warmth, generosity, and compassion. Peter Harris taught me pretty much everything I needed to know about being a campaign manager, and Joel Johnson and Kevin Bruns (whom I later hired for John's 1992 campaign) were adept and highly competent colleagues who made my job easier.

~

Of the many other candidates I've worked with over the years, the late Jerry Springer was in a class by himself. I count myself fortunate for having gotten to know him, along with Jene Galvin and the late Mike Ford and his wife, Sally, who comprised the rest of our very small team.

Joel Hyatt, who now lives in California and is an eminently successful entrepreneur, was a very good candidate who had the misfortune of running for the Senate in a very bad year. I am grateful for his continuing friendship.

Other Ohio politicians—some of whom I worked with and some of whom I worked against—earned my admiration and entered public service for all the right reasons. Among them are former Ohio governors Richard Celeste, Ted Strickland, Bob Taft, and John Kasich; former Senator Sherrod Brown; and congressional representatives or state officeholders like Marcy Kaptur, Lee Fisher, Gene Branstool, Dennis Kucinich, Bob Shamansky, Dennis Eckart, Ed Feighan, Asher Sweeney, Tom Moyer, and Betty Montgomery who, along with the late GOP state chairman Bob Bennett, were class acts who fought hard but fairly. Jim Ruvolo was probably the most effective Democratic state chairman in Ohio history, and Jerry Austin is one of the smartest (and most quotable) political operatives I've ever known. Dave Regan and Bill and Tim Burga were extraordinarily talented labor leaders with whom it was always a pleasure to work. Curt Steiner and Terry Casey are gifted Republican consultants I've often battled, always respected, and am proud to call my friends.

There are many print and electronic media journalists I regularly engaged and sparred with over the years, including Mike Curtin, Colleen Marshall, Mike Thompson, Brent Larkin, Bill Hershey, Tim Miller, Sandy Theis, Joe Hallett, Mary Ann Sharkey, Tom Beres, Laura Bischoff, Tom Diemer, Jonathan Riskind, Bert de Souza, Chris Burnett, Steve Luttner, Jerry Anderson, Alan Johnson, Tom Price, Randy Wynn, Darrel Rowland, David Skolnick, Jerry Revish, Angela Pace, Michael Douglas, Ann Fisher, Henry Gomez, Howard Wilkinson, Jack Torry, Jessica Wehrman, Julie Carr Smyth, Bill Cohen, Karen Kasler, Andrew Welsh-Huggins, Keith Burris, Scott Light, Lynn Hulsey, Jessie Balmert, Mark Naymik, Jo Ingles, Mark Niquette, Jeremy Pelzer, Randy Ludlow, Tom Suddes, the late Tom Brazaitis, Chase Clements, Joe Dirck, Lee Leonard, and Mary Yost, and so many others I wish space allowed me to name. We didn't always see eye to eye and our disagreements were sometimes intense, but I never questioned your professionalism or doubted your integrity.

I also want to thank John Green, who headed the Ray Bliss Institute and taught politics at The University of Akron for many years and who encouraged me to write this book and offered a number of suggestions to make it better. I can only hope he's equally willing to disrupt his own retirement by writing another book himself.

I owe an enormous debt to the professionals at The University of Akron Press who have helped this first-time author bring his book to fruition. Director Jon Miller has made excellent suggestions and has always been honest and up front with me, as have his UA Press colleagues Brittany LaPointe and Amy Freels. I also want to acknowledge the many contributions made by my peerless copy editor, Nancy Basmajian, whose assistance has been invaluable. All of them have shown me more patience than I probably deserve.

Two of my teachers—one in high school and one in college—opened new worlds for me. At Abilene Christian University, the late Professor Gary Thompson sparked my interest in politics and government. And I am even more indebted to Emily Ackerman, my English teacher at Northwood High School. At an age and a time when I failed to take studies seriously and school counselors were actively discouraging my going to college, Emily saw a talent for writing that no one else detected. The one-woman war she waged with school administrators to get me into an Advanced Composition class changed my life. Changing lives, of course, is what good teachers often do, usually without fanfare and seldom with the recognition they deserve.

Above all, I want to thank my family: my father Ken, who passed away far too soon at the age of sixty-one, and my mother Helen, who lived with grace and dignity into her eighty-third year. The values they instilled in me and my sister, Mary-Alison, are timeless and true—and they sacrificed much to give me opportunities they never had.

My wife Vicki and our five children, Danielle, Chad, Brodie, Shane, and Carter, have been the enduring loves of my life. Those who have undertaken the challenge know that blending families is never easy and sometimes yields unexpected complications. But I remain enormously proud of the job Vicki and I did and rest secure in the conviction that our family's days of love and laughter far transcend and ultimately outweigh whatever mistakes I made along the way. Both for her countless sacrifices and for being the definition of a selfless and loving mom and stepmom from the very outset of our journey, Vicki deserves much of the credit. She has also been a phenomenal wife and a steadfast partner who has loyally stood with me through every success and every adversity for the past thirty-five years. I cannot thank her enough—nor could I love her more.

We have eleven grandchildren now, which is probably proof positive that our family should begin negotiations with the Planned Parenthood Association. But if Mackenzie, Morgan, Olivia, Sofia, Georgia, Arthur, Patrick, Liam, Harper, Brooks, and Everett grow up to be even half the parent their Grandma Vicki has been, the world will surely be a kinder and more gentle place.

Index

Photo: Danielle Skestos

Dale Butland has forty-six years of experience in government and political communications. For nearly two decades, he worked for the late US Senator (and astronaut) John Glenn, serving as his press secretary, Ohio chief of staff, and reelection campaign director. He's also worked for numerous other Ohio politicians, including US Senator Howard M. Metzenbaum and talk show host Jerry Springer. He regularly appears on several politics and public affairs television shows and is a frequent op-ed contributor to many Ohio newspapers. In 2016, his poignant remembrance of Senator Glenn, "The Last American Hero?," was published by *The New York Times*.